Shakespeare and Ecofeminist Theory

ARDEN SHAKESPEARE AND THEORY

Series Editor: Evelyn Gajowski

AVAILABLE TITLES

Shakespeare and Ecofeminist Theory Rebecca Laroche and Jennifer Munroe
Shakespeare and Economic Theory David Hawkes
Shakespeare and Ecocritical Theory Gabriel Egan
Shakespeare and New Historicist Theory Neema Parvini
Shakespeare and Psychoanalytic Theory Carolyn Brown

FORTHCOMING TITLES

Shakespeare and Cultural Materialist Theory Christopher Marlow
Shakespeare and Feminist Theory Marianne Novy
Shakespeare and Film Theory Scott Hollifield
Shakespeare and Postcolonial Theory Jyotsna Singh
Shakespeare and Posthumanist Theory Karen Raber
Shakespeare and Presentist Theory Evelyn Gajowski
Shakespeare and Queer Theory Melissa Sanchez
Shakespeare and Race Theory Arthur L. Little, Jr.

Shakespeare and Ecofeminist Theory

Rebecca Laroche and Jennifer Munroe

Bloomsbury Arden Shakespeare
An imprint of Bloomsbury Publishing Plc

B L O O M S B U R Y
LONDON · OXFORD · NEW YORK · NEW DELHI · SYDNEY

Bloomsbury Arden Shakespeare
An imprint of Bloomsbury Publishing Plc

Imprint previously known as Arden Shakespeare

50 Bedford Square	1385 Broadway
London	New York
WC1B 3DP	NY 10018
UK	USA

www.bloomsbury.com

BLOOMSBURY, THE ARDEN SHAKESPEARE and the Diana logo are trademarks of Bloomsbury Publishing Plc

First published 2017

© Rebecca Laroche and Jennifer Munroe, 2017

Rebecca Laroche and Jennifer Munroe have asserted their rights under the Copyright, Designs and Patents Act, 1988, to be identified as authors of this work.

All rights reserved. No part of this publication may be reproduced or transmitted in any form or by any means, electronic or mechanical, including photocopying, recording, or any information storage or retrieval system, without prior permission in writing from the publishers.

No responsibility for loss caused to any individual or organization acting on or refraining from action as a result of the material in this publication can be accepted by Bloomsbury or the author.

British Library Cataloguing-in-Publication Data
A catalogue record for this book is available from the British Library.

ISBN: HB: 978-1-4725-9046-6
PB: 978-1-4725-9045-9
ePDF: 978-1-4725-9048-0
ePub: 978-1-4725-9047-3

Library of Congress Cataloging-in-Publication Data
A catalog record for this book is available from the Library of Congress.

Series: Shakespeare and Theory

Series cover design by Sutchinda Rangsi Thompson
Cover image © Brownstock/Alamy Stock Photo

Typeset by Fakenham Prepress Solutions, Fakenham, Norfolk NR21 8NN

For Lynne Dickson Bruckner, who brought us here

CONTENTS

Series Editor's Preface ix
Acknowledgements xii
Preface: Communities, collaborations and chaos xiv
   The Process of the book xvi

Introduction: Ecofeminism and the seeds of time 1
   Ecofeminism past and present 2
   Ecofeminism in/and early modern studies 11

1 Ecofeminism matters 17
   Domesticated beings 18
   Knowing things 22
   A substance of subject–objects 26
   Historical practice and present crisis 32

2 Of mouseholes and housefires: Transcorporeal domesticity 39
   'Noysome and pestilent things' 42
   Pest control: The scratching cat and 'the smallest monstrous mouse' 51
   (Beyond) pest control: Fleas, flies and other creeping creatures 58
   Between small and great, soft and fierce: The hearth 63
   After the fire 73

3 How we know any thing 77
  Nothing is everything 78
  Unknowability 89
  'Howe'er you come to know it' 98
  The power of and in uncertainty 103

4 The dynamic object 105
  The indifference of stone 105
  Dynamism in the garden 109
  (Boys as) women as plants 117
  Petrarch in the produce aisle 128

Conclusion: Nature, stir: Ecofeminists in the archive 131
  Healing nature 131
  Living nature 140

Appendix: Excavating nature 143
Notes 147
Bibliography 171
Index 185

SERIES EDITOR'S PREFACE

'Asking questions about literary texts – that's literary criticism. Asking "Which questions shall we ask about literary texts?" – that's literary theory.' So goes my explanation of the current state of English studies, and Shakespeare studies, in my never-ending attempt to demystify, and simplify, theory for students in my classrooms. Another way to put it is that theory is a systematic account of the nature of literature, the act of writing, and the act of reading.

One of the primary responsibilities of any academic discipline – whether in the natural sciences, the social sciences, or the humanities – is to examine its methodologies and tools of analysis. Particularly at a time of great theoretical ferment, such as that which has characterized English studies, and Shakespeare studies, in recent years, it is incumbent upon scholars in a given discipline to provide such reflection and analysis. We all construct meanings in Shakespeare's texts and culture. Shouldering responsibility for our active role in constructing meanings in literary texts, moreover, constitutes a theoretical stance. To the extent that we examine our own critical premises and operations, that theoretical stance requires reflection on our part. It requires honesty, as well. It is thereby a fundamentally radical act. All critical analysis puts into practice a particular set of theoretical premises. Theory occurs from a particular standpoint. There is no critical practice that is somehow devoid of theory. There is no critical practice that is not implicated in theory. A common-sense, transparent encounter with any text is thereby impossible. Indeed, to the extent that theory requires us to question anew that with which we thought we were familiar, that which we thought we understood, theory constitutes a critique of common sense.

Since the advent of postmodernism, the discipline of English studies has undergone a seismic shift. And the discipline of Shakespeare studies has been at the epicentre of this shift. Indeed, it has been Shakespeare scholars who have played a major role in several of the theoretical and critical developments (e.g., new historicism, cultural materialism, presentism) that have shaped the discipline of English studies in recent years. Yet a comprehensive scholarly analysis of these crucial developments has yet to be done, and is long overdue. As the first series to foreground analysis of contemporary theoretical developments in the discipline of Shakespeare studies, *Arden Shakespeare and Theory* aims to fill a yawning gap.

To the delight of some and the chagrin of others, since 1980 or so, theory has dominated Shakespeare studies. *Arden Shakespeare and Theory* focuses on the state of the art at the outset of the twenty-first century. For the first time, it provides a comprehensive analysis of the theoretical developments that are emerging at the present moment, as well as those that are dominant or residual in Shakespeare studies.

Each volume in the series aims to offer the reader the following components: to provide a clear definition of a particular theory; to explain its key concepts; to trace its major developments, theorists, and critics; to perform a reading of a Shakespeare text; to elucidate a specific theory's intersection with or relationship to other theories; to situate it in the context of contemporary political, social, and economic developments; to analyze its significance in Shakespeare studies; and to suggest resources for further investigation. Authors of individual volumes thereby attempt to strike a balance, bringing their unique expertise, experience, and perspectives to bear upon particular theories while simultaneously fulfilling the common purpose of the series. Individual volumes in the series are devoted to elucidating particular theoretical perspectives, such as cultural materialism, ecocriticism, ecofeminism, economic theory, feminism, film theory, new historicism, postcoloniality, posthumanism, presentism, psychoanalysis, queer theory and race theory.

Arden Shakespeare and Theory aims to enable scholars, teachers, and students alike to define their own theoretical strategies and refine their own critical practices. And students have as much at stake in these theoretical and critical enterprises – in the reading and the writing practices that characterize our discipline – as do scholars and teachers. Janus-like, the series looks forward as well as backward, serving as an inspiration and a guide for new work in Shakespeare studies at the outset of the twenty-first century, on the one hand, and providing a retrospective analysis of the intellectual labour that has been accomplished in recent years, on the other.

To return to the beginning: what is at stake in our reading of literary texts? Once we come to understand the various ways in which theory resonates with not only Shakespeare's texts, and literary texts, but the so-called 'real' world – the world outside the world of the mind, the world outside the world of academia – then we come to understand that theory is capable of powerfully enriching not only our reading of Shakespeare's texts, and literary texts, but our lives.

I am indebted to David Avital, Publisher at Bloomsbury Academic, who was instrumental in developing the idea of the *Arden Shakespeare and Theory Series*. I am also grateful to Margaret Bartley, Publisher or Arden Shakespeare, for her guidance and support throughout the development of this Series.

Evelyn Gajowski
Series Editor
University of Nevada, Las Vegas

ACKNOWLEDGEMENTS

This book is the product of numerous collaborations. Most immediately, we thank Evelyn Gajowski, whose generous invitation to write a monograph dedicated to ecofeminist theory made our own collaboration possible. And a special and most heartfelt thanks to Lynne Dickson Bruckner, to whom we dedicate this book for a number of reasons. Lynne helped us put a name to the work we had been doing for some time, but she also exemplifies the foundational qualities of ecofeminist work, exuding compassion for all living things, human and nonhuman alike. Our classrooms in spring 2015 served as the medium to germinate the ideas that fill this book. Therefore we offer appreciation to our students in the Shakespeare and Ecofeminist Theory classes at the University of Colorado, Colorado Springs, and University of North Carolina, Charlotte, who came along with us for the ride, almost always in good humour, and who themselves became co-producers of this project. To the many seminar leaders and participants at the Shakespeare Association of America (SAA) meetings who have helped us refine and clarify our ideas in recent years, we offer our gratitude. And for their insightful readings of in-progress chapters and their central role in our intellectual and social community, we thank Keith Botelho and Debapriya Sarkar.

This book would not have been possible without our co-Steering Committee members of the Early Modern Recipes Online Collective (EMROC) – Elaine Leong, Hillary Nunn, Lisa Smith and Amy Tigner – whose camaraderie and intellectual support have sustained us. We are also appreciative of the officers of the UNC Charlotte Early Modern Paleography Society (EMPS) – Breanne Weber, Kailan Sindelar, Taryn

Dollings, Robin Kello and Nadia Clifton – whose commitment to early modern recipe books has helped energize their student community and inspire the scholarship we present here. We thank the University of North Carolina, Charlotte, for research support in the form of a Reassignment of Duties during spring 2016 as well as the University of Colorado, Colorado Springs, for ongoing research support. And, finally, to Alan White and Ruth E. Lambert, whose love and patience are a source of strength and a reminder that we never embark on these things alone.

Note about transcription: all manuscript transcriptions unless otherwise indicated are by the authors, using semi-diplomatic conventions. The exception is that we are not retaining line breaks from the original manuscripts.

PREFACE: COMMUNITIES, COLLABORATIONS AND CHAOS

But come thy ways, we'll go along together ...[1]

Organisms are ecosystems of genomes, consortia, communities, partly digested dinners, mortal boundary formations.[2]

[I]f we are to champion the need for environmental humanities today, it must be a version of this field that self-reflexively acknowledges and even nurtures its own contradictions, variances, and necessary open-endedness.[3]

Motivated by the urgency of the human influence on climate change, literary studies has in recent years turned its attention to the relationship between the human and nonhuman natural worlds. Just as scholarship in studies of race, class and gender has informed and been informed by contemporary movements as well as literary and popular texts, so too has our current ecological crisis catalysed an interest in interrogating intersections between environmental issues (of the past and present) and writing. One area of enquiry that has gained momentum in recent decades, ecocriticism, considers these questions, but *Shakespeare and Ecofeminist Theory* focuses on another field that does so. Too often relegated to being a subset of ecocriticism, ecofeminism has a scholarly history of its own, as we will discuss in the Introduction – one that arguably precedes and whose interests extend beyond ecocriticism. Ecofeminism takes as its primary concern the way the relationship between the human and nonhuman is both material and cultural, but it also investigates how this relationship is inherently entangled with issues of gender equity and environmental justice.

Shakespeare and Ecofeminist Theory continues the work that ecofeminist scholars have begun as it theorizes the relationship between the human and nonhuman natural worlds, with a particular eye to these issues, and it establishes a history of ecofeminist scholarship both within and relevant to early modern studies. Arguing that a consideration of material practice, where culture and 'nature' meet, proves an especially useful way to illuminate these issues, this book emphasizes how we might understand Shakespeare as immersed in an environment where men, women, animals and plants lived necessarily in relations that were at once symbiotic and in tension. And it demonstrates how this lived experience was not simply understood by way of differences between humans and nonhumans but was shaped by gender difference as well.

Here, we consider a variety and range of genres in Shakespeare's writings. Rather than focusing on one or two plays as they relate to a particular issue of relevance to ecofeminism, we treat multiple texts in each body chapter to demonstrate how the issues at stake apply broadly to Shakespeare's corpus; we also show how unconventional juxtapositions of texts (e.g. *Macbeth* with *All's Well That Ends Well*) reveal new ways to read his plays that would be of interest to any scholar of Shakespeare and early modern England, not only those with an eye to the green. In so doing, this book troubles and reconceives familiar categories – domestic/wild, natural/supernatural, animate/inanimate – to provide fresh insights about early modern texts in general, and Shakespeare, ecocritical, feminist and ecofeminist studies in particular. *Shakespeare and Ecofeminist Theory* illuminates how ecofeminism provides a means of not only complicating certain trajectories that are dominant within current strands of ecocriticism, but also extending insights that have been garnered through feminist enquiry. While previous feminist readings of Shakespeare's plays have focused on objectification, subjugation and empowerment in social spheres, this book shows how ecofeminism applies questions of social justice and cultural domination as they relate to interactions with the living environment.

By writing a monograph that couples Shakespeare with ecofeminist theory, we argue that uniting the interests of 'eco' and 'feminist' scholarship will help us understand something that we cannot by investigating either of these approaches independent of one other. In combining the concerns of ecocriticism and feminism, we, like Noël Sturgeon, emphasize how 'ecofeminism', as a term and a theoretical approach, 'indicates a double political intervention; of environmentalism into feminism and feminism into environmentalism'.[4] Thus bringing together these two approaches enriches each and yields new readings. This book, therefore, serves as just such an intervention, as we believe that putting these two fields in dialogue offers ways to think about multiple and related forms of subjugation at once rather than treating them as if they might be separated.

The process of the book

While we go into more detail about individual chapters and elaborate on their relevance to ecofeminist theory and their contribution to Shakespeare and early modern studies in Chapter 1 – the plan of the book, as it were – we would like to spend time here elaborating on our process. For co-authoring this book was not simply an accident; it is the realization of what lies at our theoretical and practical core – that valuing collaboration and polyvocality best illustrates what we believe is one of the greatest contributions of ecofeminism.

This book draws on the import of such collaborations: the ecological, physiological, historical, textual, political, intellectual, social. Within the fields of feminist and ecological literary studies, these have been variously called alliances, networks, exchanges, assemblages, all indicating shared space, time and embodiment. As we detail more at length in the Introduction, ecofeminism (and its theoretical foundations) has a rich history of political alliances among women whereby they unify around, even as they might also resist, their associations with the nonhuman natural world. From the microbiome within our guts, to the air we breathe, to the food we process and digest, we are linked in ways that exceed our wilful selves and that have collateral effects (both negative and positive) for those with whom we share this planet.

Underlying ecofeminist work is a desire to redress inequalities that result not only from forms of domination that subject women, colonial Others, racial Others, the poor and nonhumans to destructive practices, but also those that might well appear to have the best interests of the most vulnerable men, women and nonhumans at heart. Some have criticized the 'sustainability' movement itself,[5] and perhaps rightly so, for being a white middle-to-upper-class endeavour, one that retains only at its margins some of the very constituents (human and nonhuman) that are, or will be, most compromised by global climate change and other effects of global industrialization. We might consider scrapping the term 'sustainability', or at least the romantic, pastoral notions associated with it, as Steve Mentz suggests, even if doing so 'need not mean consigning ourselves to an unintelligible ecosphere'[6]; Mentz proposes we might begin by 'letting go of harmony', or at least the sense of harmony aligned with our sense of the world as pastoral ideal.[7] But 'harmony' may be a useful term to keep, as it might serve as a corrective for the stasis 'sustainability' implies (as so many critique) and move us instead towards embracing a multiplicity that works towards a robustly diverse and interactive whole. To this idea of harmony, we add the notion of chaos, divested of its negative connotations, to suggest how disruptions and change catalyse such robustness, such that we value multiple and perpetually emerging collaborations and communities.

The ecofeminist theory we practise throughout this book has been influenced by all of these, and our co-authorship is an expression of the rich, harmonic chaos that characterizes the day-to-day comings and goings in and with the world we occupy. At the heart of such collaborations, including our own as co-authors, is a persistent belief that in experiencing the world as a collective we are made better than by a wrong-headed insistence on the primacy of the 'I'. The notion of harmonic chaos also serves as an organizing principle for this book. As practitioners of environmental humanities work, we aim to bring together ways of thinking about the social and the natural here in our work on ecofeminist theory and Shakespeare; but we also believe that in so doing, as one of the epigraphs with which we opened this chapter, we might well 'self-reflexively acknowledge[ ] and even nurture[ ]' our 'own contradictions, variances, and necessary open-endedness'.[8] In our application of ecofeminist theory to Shakespeare's writings, we take such a mantra seriously.

As a result, we have approached the writing of each chapter to reflect the openness with which we believe ecofeminist theory asks us to embrace our experience with the world we co-inhabit. In places, we offer examples of elaborated close readings of a small number of texts by Shakespeare using ecofeminist theory to unfold new ways of reading them, as you will see in Chapter 3 in particular. But in the spirit of experimentation, of valuing the open-endedness that comes from engaging with the unfamiliar, we also offer less conventional ways of reading and thinking about how one might apply a theoretical model like ecofeminism. And so, strewn throughout the pages that follow, you will find approaches to Shakespeare using ecofeminist theory that alternate between deep readings and ruminations, traversing the boundaries of household spaces, the human mouth and skin, the garden wall, boiling water and earth's rich humus, to name just a few. In Chapter 1, we detail how certain premises related to ecofeminist theory help us read not only the particulars of Shakespeare's texts with fresh perspectives, but also how such ideas might unlock new approaches to early modern material history: the domestic, knowledge-making, and subject/object relations.

Throughout the book, we couple readings of Shakespeare with other texts to expose the subterranean layers of literary and material, ecological and social, and other collaborative exchanges. In places, we move back and forth between close readings of Shakespeare and those of other early modern texts to show how ecofeminist theory might collectively and mutually inform a more holistic sense of early modernity. Chapter 2, for instance, thinks about the imperative of domestication for both women and nonhumans in plays ranging from *The Taming of the Shrew* to *Othello* and from gardening manuals (like Gervase Markham's) to women's manuscript recipe books. In other moments, we focus on more protracted readings such as in Chapter 3's discussions of Shakespeare's *King Lear*, *All's Well That Ends Well* and *Macbeth*, and these readings show how ecofeminist theory yields new ways to see these plays that, in turn, also speak more broadly to our concerns as early modern scholars. And Chapter 4 begins with *The Winter's Tale*, then ventures through the Sonnets, *All's Well That Ends Well*, *Twelfth Night* and *As You Like It*, and back to *The Winter's Tale*, and all the while accompanying such lofty literary texts are such palpable nonhuman things as stone, roses, violets, daffodils and strawberries. Because our role as ecofeminist scholars of Shakespeare and early modern England necessitates that we straddle the past and the present, as we think through these topics in each chapter as they relate to literary and other texts from centuries ago, we understand them as well through our own contemporary moment. And so, along with a hobgoblin's warning to rake the coals, you will find the Colorado wild fires of 2002, or the 'ugly fruit' movement of today with Petrarchan love poetry, or a recipe to stop a nosebleed with Zika virus, or Helena's curing of the King with our growing cultural tension between STEM – Science, Technology, Engineering and Mathematics – and the Humanities. These travel through and across time, hand in hand, their sensibilities never entirely unique, though ever-morphing into that which each generation recognizes as its own.

Introduction: Ecofeminism and the seeds of time

> *By slow violence I mean a violence that occurs gradually and out of sight, a violence of delayed destruction that is dispersed across time and space, an attritional violence that is typically not viewed as violence at all.*[1]

> *Why shouldn't feminist theorists welcome a political discourse that interrogates the equation of women with nature and examines the political consequences of that equation not just for women but for nature as well?*[2]

In this introduction, we trace the history of ecofeminism, its application by literary scholars and its development within Shakespeare and early modern studies. Hardly just an offshoot of environmentalism or ecocriticism (its literary studies counterpart), ecofeminism has always been a distinct field in its own right. Annette Kolodny's *The Lay of the Land: Metaphor as Experience and History in American Life and Letters* (1975) appeared at roughly the same time as William Reuckert first proposed to study literature alongside ecology, and the term 'ecocriticism' was used to name the field two decades later.[3] While ecocriticism and ecofeminism have overlapping interests and developed in parallel in some ways, they each have their own unique trajectory. We show how early modern ecofeminist scholarship has been informed by ecofeminist work in other historical periods and literatures, especially American literature and the history of science, where ecofeminist scholars have had an influential presence for decades. Ecofeminist scholarship in Shakespeare has drawn from this work, but it has also forged its own way by building on the work of activists, scientists and philosophers. Here, we sift through some of the complicated, historically contingent aspects of the alignment of the categories 'women' and 'nature' to show how they need not necessarily be negative, 'dirty' associations, if you will, but neither need we understand them to be intrinsically linked. We focus instead on the import of studying how women got their hands dirty, how their material connection with earth – with the earthworms, swallows and snails from which they made regenerative waters and the sage, rosemary and radishes that sustained their diets – and its representation in Shakespeare is rich terrain for exploring alternative ways of thinking about his dramas and the rest of early modern literature.

Ecofeminism past and present

Like ecocriticism, ecofeminism has roots in the environmentalist movement of the 1970s, but it has its own developed and unique set of interests and applications. The term 'ecofeminism', coined by Françoise d'Eaubonne in her work *La Feminisme ou la Mort* in 1974, was more broadly used at least as early as 1980 in reference to the 'Women and Life on Earth: Ecofeminism in the 1980s' conference at Amherst.[4] The 'Ecofeminist Perspectives: Culture, Nature, Theory' conference at the University of Southern California in 1987 marked what Noël Sturgeon describes as 'the point where the word ecofeminism began to be used outside the antimilitarist movement to describe a politics that attempted to combine feminism, environmentalism, antiracism, animal liberation, anticolonialism, antimilitarism, and non-traditional spiritualities'.[5] Ecofeminists thus have ties to environmental justice activists and shared motivations with those who work in postcolonialism, race studies, gender studies and environmental studies.

In this way, ecofeminism has obvious alliances with both the environmental movement and second-wave feminism, and its practitioners have often sought to bridge the two. In the 1970s, and even before, politically oriented work appeared that articulated the links between environmentalism and feminism, such as Rachel Carson's *Silent Spring* (1962), Rosemary Radford Ruether's *New Woman/New Earth* (1975), Susan Griffin's *Woman and Nature: The Roaring Inside Her* (1980), Elizabeth Dodson Gray's *Green Paradise Lost* (1979), Carolyn Merchant's *The Death of Nature* (1980) and multiple writings by Val Plumwood.[6] Leonie Caldecott and Stephanie Leland's *Reclaim the Earth: Women Speak Out for Life on Earth* (1983) and Karen Warren's *Ecological Feminism* (1994) were among the first anthologies in ecofeminist philosophy. Drawing on the way environmentalists called attention to the increasingly visible negative consequences of industrialism and development, and stemming from how feminists located destructive practices of multiple dominant systems (patriarchal and colonial endeavour, for instance), ecofeminist practitioners sought to interrogate their associations. Ecofeminism, however, developed its own vocabulary and its own approach to these concerns.

In particular, ecofeminist theorists and scholars have an interest in analysing the overlapping territory between environmental criticism and feminist and gender criticism. If, as Victoria Davion insists, 'there is an important link between the domination of women and the domination of nature, and that an understanding of one is aided by an understanding of the other', then we would benefit from a consideration of these related forms of domination.[7] A focus on linked forms of domination is characteristic of ecofeminism, then, although analyses of their relationship have taken multiple forms. Within ecofeminism, historians of science and scientists have approached this problem by aiming to destabilize the nature/culture dualism and its attendant implications for gendered power relations. Carolyn Merchant's *The Death of Nature* (1980) and Donna Haraway's 'A Cyborg Manifesto' (1984) were both seminal works, even if quite different in their focus and approach. Merchant's historical accounting linked the rise of scientific discourse in the seventeenth century with an understanding of women and nature as passive objects of male knowledge. And Haraway's cyborg serves as an icon of the blurring of the interrelated binaries human/nonhuman and male/female and a means by which we might interrogate their mutual constructedness. In the fields of science and philosophy, ecofeminists have argued that 'objectivity' itself is a construct that divests both women and Nature of agency and results in the dominance of human over nonhuman, man over woman. Val Plumwood's *Environmental Culture*, like Merchant's *Death of Nature*, looks to the origins of scientific discourse, though Plumwood applies her critique of what she calls 'monologic' systems (as opposed to 'dialogic') to today as well.[8] Vandana Shiva, an ecofeminist physicist and activist, interrogates objectivity in the context of progressivist notions about 'development' as she argues that dominant (and 'masculinist') modes of agricultural production are themselves built upon what ecofeminists have viewed as fundamentally destructive perspectives and technologies with respect to our human interactions with the nonhuman world.[9] Dominant technologies and scientific discourses that propagate 'objectivity', she argues, turn both women and nature 'into passive objects, to be used and exploited for the uncontrolled and uncontrollable desires of alienated man'.[10]

Those working in ecofeminist literary studies (or environmentalist feminist literary studies) have sought in particular to unpack the way that women and land are often linked – for instance, how 'virgin' territory simultaneously evokes both the imagined as-yet claimed geographic territory and as-yet penetrated female body. In the past two decades, publications such as Stacy Alaimo's *Undomesticated Ground: Recasting Nature as Feminine Space* (2000) have troubled such associations. Alaimo and others have shown how the link between women and land may well have served to (re)imagine them both as property and as terrain to be inhabited and conquered, but it also afforded women outlets for reimagining potential alternative avenues to power. Ecofeminist scholarship within literary studies, especially following the 'linguistic turn' of the 1990s within gender studies, has often taken as its purpose not the reinforcement of the woman/land connection that underscores the culture/nature binary, but rather a progressive and transcultural deconstruction of such associations even as it seeks to historicize its material practical application.

Shakespeare and Ecofeminist Theory considers the interplay between these forms of subjugation, what sociologist Jason Moore terms the 'socio-ecological' – or the 'bundled' qualities that both feminism and ecocriticism aim to unfold independently.[11] Of interest to Moore, as with the ecofeminist theory we bring to bear here, is the utility of investigating the interplay between social and historical systems and what we tend to call natural ones, to interrogate the mutually subjecting forces of androcentrism and anthropocentrism. But we maintain that with a focus on the 'socio-ecological', ecofeminism offers a way to talk about these multiple forms of subjugation in ways that are unique. Feminist scholars have attended to such power relations for some time, producing excellent work to date, both in early modern studies and beyond, but their focus has been more the 'socio' than the 'ecological'. However, since the subjection of women to men has historically been linked to that of nonhumans to humans, looking only at the former risks inadvertently reifying the latter. Karen Warren argues, for instance, that one without the other provides only a partial picture, that each has something to teach the other: 'an environmental perspective is *theoretically* necessary to feminism', and uniting environmentalism and feminism, as ecofeminism aims to do, addresses 'the conceptual and structural interconnections between *all* forms of domination'.[12] That is, the subjection of women to men and nonhuman things to human are fundamentally linked to ideas and practices that would be productively interrogated together.

The 'material turn' within feminist and gender studies thus offers a promising direction upon which ecofeminist work might build. Moving away from the social constructivism of the 'linguistic turn' of 1990s feminist and gender studies, materialist feminists have directed our attention to how bodies, even physical environments, indeed matter itself, are linked; and how power relations are palpable material expressions in everyday practice as well as abstract impositions upon individuals and groups. Not surprisingly, some practitioners of materialist feminism cross over into posthumanism as well, as they take into account how nonhumans, not just humans (or women) figure in these material relationships.

To say that ecofeminists have redressed multiple forms of subjugation, then, is not to claim that work for them alone. However, our approach in *Shakespeare and Ecofeminist Theory* begins at what we believe to be the limits (at least thus far) of both ecocriticism (and posthumanism) and feminism and combines them to foster dialogue across both these fields and maximize the potential of each. Feminist and queer studies' deconstructive moves *vis-à-vis* subjectivity, especially the querying of subject positions that constitute 'subject' versus 'object', have given us an entry point into this conversation. And posthumanism has as well, with its interest in 'thing power' and the agency of what had hitherto been understood as passive – that is, objects, or 'things'. At the same time, posthumanists tend to elide questions of social justice in order to query a broader notion of anthropocentrism; their moves often default to andro- and ethnocentric modes of seeing. Ecofeminism understands speciesist discourse to be entangled with racism, sexism, ableism and classism, and therefore not to be bracketed, to be discussed in another forum or to be considered later, or, worse yet, as that which has already been articulated. To ignore these entanglements is to risk complicity in the sort of 'slow violence' Rob Nixon describes, which renders their destructive effects invisible, insignificant.

Our particular ecofeminist focus on materialism in this book, then, builds on but is necessarily distinguished from feminist as well as the recent posthumanist work on early modern literature and culture. Such posthumanist work often turns to Bruno Latour's ostensibly democratizing call for a bicameral 'parliament' of things, one that would see humans and nonhumans as co-actants in an ontologically co-producing array.[13] The posthumanist scholarship that emanates from it tends to emphasize a retheorizing of humans and nonhumans as collectively comprised 'things' rather than distinct entities. Scholars of posthumanism have usefully reoriented notions of subjectivity that privilege human cognition – following a Cartesian model – to emphasize instead bodily and intellectual formations of selfhood.[14] But in the process of asserting humans and nonhumans to be mutually constituted 'things', such scholarship has also tended to de-emphasize the power relations that come into play in such mutual co-constitution.[15] However, to ignore these power relations, we insist, risks reifying an idealized version of 'things' seemingly immune to the harsh realities of social and environmental injustice. 'Nature' in this sense teeters on the edge of becoming simply an imagined new version of what is apparently interrogated – not 'things' at all, but a rarefied representation of them. Or, as Alaimo puts it, such 'idealization of nature as a pure field apart from social struggles' might well serve to reinforce the very power relations that Latour's 'parliament' ostensibly aims to resist, as such a 'pure field' in turn 'constitutes [nature] as the ideal site for playing out – while repressing – anxieties about threats to white male middle- to upper-class social power.'[16]

Because posthumanist work has tended to elide race, class and gender, it is not surprising that posthumanist scholars have too often not cited the work of ecofeminists who have been focusing on these categories for decades.[17] The chapters that follow in this book aim to redress such elision. We employ ecofeminism as a way to theorize the relationship between human and nonhuman 'things', but we show how they are intertwined with the matrix of power in early modern England. In so doing, we answer Karen Barad's call to unite posthumanist retheorizations of the co-agentic qualities of 'things' with a genuine attention to how power relations are part of their co-creation. Or, as Barad writes, 'Any proposal for a new political collective' that might help realize the ideal Latour articulates 'must take account of not merely the practices that produce distinctions between the human and the nonhuman but the *practices through which their differential constitution is produced*'.[18] And so, as identity politics serve as one example of such 'differential constitution', a 'new political collective' would do well to account for them as well.

One way we might account for such 'differential constitution' is to re-evaluate how we historicize the early modern period to further complicate our understanding of human–nonhuman relations. The Anthropocene, a now-familiar term used to isolate the moment at which human interaction with the nonhuman world took a markedly destructive turn, has served to help ecocritics contextualize the historical roots of our current ecological crises. But this term also relies on a notion of 'human' that operates as a universal marker and generically includes men and women from a variety of backgrounds (race, class, etc.). At the same time, scholars have documented how all men and women did not participate in, benefit from or suffer equally (either then or now) because of the increased mechanization of industrialism. The term Anthropocene thus elides such inequalities and inadvertently reinforces the race, class and gender dominance that has been inextricably linked to the relationship between humans and nonhumans following industrialization. Instead, as Moore suggests, we might reorient our thinking to differentiate such inequalities by deploying a different term – for him, it is 'Capitalocene' – that redresses the 'fictitious human unity' inherent in the term Anthropocene with a focus on the disparate material realities and practices of men and women across time. 'The issue', writes Moore, 'is not one of anthropogenic-drivers – presuming a fictitious human unity – but of the relations of capital and capitalist power'; or, the 'new law of value that reconfigured uncommodified human and extra-human natures (slaves, forests, soil) in servitude to labor productivity and the commodity'.[19] To recuperate a fuller sense of how this played out in early modern England requires that we go beyond simply theorizing these relations with broad strokes ('human' and 'nonhuman') to historicizing their particulars and doing so with a focus on that/those which/who were positioned in such servitude. We must, that is, seek to untangle their attendant power relations – especially gender, race and class.

In light of recent posthumanist and feminist/gender studies work, however, untangling such relations is a complicated proposition because it means also drawing attention to an association between women and nature that has made ecofeminism vulnerable to claims of essentialism. These claims have come from both environmental criticism and feminism, ecofeminism's would-be partners, and have resulted too often in a rejection by both – a 'flight from nature', as it were. This need not be so. To acknowledge the historical particulars of women's association with nonhuman nature is not to reify an essential connection between the two. In fact, we would argue the opposite: attending to them is to *resist* essentialism; to ignore them would be to essentialize human experience at the expense of a fuller sense of its rich diversity. Women were, as historical work in the early modern period punctuates, associated with nonhuman nature in ways that were simultaneously marginalizing and empowering. But by asserting as much we do not mean to suggest that women are inherently connected to the earth. Part of ecofeminism's history is an embracing of 'earth goddess' identity,[20] but this is not the core of ecofeminism's project, nor does it represent the majority perspective – or ours.

Rather than reiterating such essentialist connections between women and nonhuman nature, we trouble their historical associations even as we expose how women sometimes used them to their advantage. In the interest of a broader project of reconstructing the embeddedness of men and women with/in nonhuman nature it is critical we also attend to the ways that women and nonhuman nature have been historically aligned. Our application of ecofeminist theory throughout this book illustrates how we need not settle for either-or propositions – *either* we theorize 'nature' absent power relations, which leads to accusations of essentialism, *or* we theorize gendered power relations absent 'nature', which seemingly liberates us from the essentialist shackles. The chapters that follow provide readings of Shakespeare that show how neither a flight from nor a flight to nature provides a full picture of early modern life or thinking. We confront the historical essentialism that articulated the association of women with nonhuman nature as we aim to resist essentialism, to posit alternative readings of this history, and to deconstruct categories that have legitimated multiple forms of subjection derived from it.

In order to complicate such historical essentialism, as well as the potential dismissal of ecofeminism as inherently essentialist today, we focus here on the material power relations that permeated early modern life. Such a material 'turn' takes as its theoretical base some of the most relevant recent work within both feminist and ecocritical studies to produce a 'situated theorizing' that 'dwells precisely at the places where the discourses of nature are implicated in classism, sexism, racism, and heterosexism'. 'Such situated theorizing, operating through a kind of grounded immersion rather than bodiless flight', writes Alaimo, 'is not only appropriate for environmental feminisms but for all feminisms that refuse Cartesian models of knowledge, agency, and subjectivity.'[21] To theorize in a situated way exposes how intersecting discourses of domination related to class, gender and race are neither accidental nor merely secondary to human–nonhuman relations.

We trouble the historically essentialized links between women and nature that have underwritten their joint subjugation even as we are interested in acknowledging (and revaluing) the social, linguistic and material practices in which the perceived relationship between women and nature might result in more beneficial ecological and social relations today. Our acknowledgment of the historical alignment between women and nature should therefore not be mistaken for an assertion of its *a priori* existence; rather, we, like so many other ecofeminist scholars, aim to uncover the often (though not always) damaging association of women and nature in order to expose its constructedness as well as its practical applications and implications for women's experiences – the constraints it placed upon women as well as how women drew upon those constraints to empower themselves and others.

Ecofeminism in/and early modern studies

Ecofeminist scholarship in early modern/Shakespeare studies to date has taken up this charge, even if it has at times met with surprising resistance from the very people who might otherwise be its potential allies. When discussion turned towards questions of gender in a recent SAA – Shakespeare Association of America – seminar on 'the nonhuman' in which we participated, an exasperated seminar member, after drawing deep breath, blurted out in frustration, 'Aren't we beyond identity politics?' This participant's response underscores why ecofeminist (and feminist) work is necessary to early modern studies as well as the resistance we and others have met when we have done it. Given the turn within ecostudies – and posthumanism in particular – away from a theorizing of gender related to human/nonhuman embeddedness, and the kneejerk response to ecofeminism as 'essentialist' (not to mention the assertion that we are post-identity politics), it is not surprising that work that self-identifies as 'ecofeminist' within early modern studies has thus far been limited to only a handful of scholars.

Important early work in early modern ecofeminist studies includes Jeanne Addison Roberts's *The Shakespearean Wild: Geography, Genus, and Gender* (1994), Sylvia Bowerbank's *Speaking for Nature: Women and Ecologies of Early Modern*

England (2004) and Diane McColley's *Milton's Eve* (1983). Roberts was the first to elucidate associations between women and nature in Shakespeare, while McColley has been instrumental in (re)turning us to Milton's writings to think in particular about the relationship between Eve and the nonhuman world. Bowerbank's *Speaking for Nature,* a book that informed our co-edited collection *Ecofeminist Approaches to Early Modernity,* approached the woman–nature connection by repositioning women as subjects, rather than just represented objects, in the conversation. More recently, and in a more self-declared way, scholars have taken up the theoretical questions related to a feminized Nature and have offered ecofeminist/feminist ecocritical readings of Shakespeare that illustrate the very principles we propose here. Lynne Bruckner's powerful 'N/nature and the Difference "She" Makes', for instance, argues for an 'ecofeminist reclamation of N/nature' that also 'take[s] into account the often troubling and gendered supplementary that this word carries'.[22] Bruckner compellingly demonstrates how 'The symmetry of woman-nature provides ... a historically based subject position that disrupts the human/nature or reason/nature dualities [that] remain culturally in place' in early modern England. Simon Estok states outright that 'Ecofeminists were doing ecocriticism long before ASLE [Association for the Study of Literature and Environment] came on the scene' as he makes connections between misogyny and his discussion of ecophobia.[23]

We (the authors of this book) have, individually and together, elaborated on the potential for ecofeminist readings of early modern texts in general and of Shakespeare in particular to do this work. *Ecofeminist Approaches to Early Modernity* assembled scholars who were thinking about the relationship between women and nature as expressed in ways that are inherently dialogic, interdependent, and it offered chapters whose subjects ranged from cooking and food preservation to grafting to travel writing to Milton's Eve. Michelle DiMeo, Rebecca Laroche, Amy Tigner and David

Goldstein all look to kitchen processes and ingredients as nodes of connectivity between women, plants and animals that are rarely romanticized, often brutal and always transactional.[24] Munroe's reading of Milton's *Paradise Lost*, on the other hand, showed how Eve's connection to earth may have made her what we might call 'ecofeminist', but her affiliation with earth itself, the blurred subject–object relations the poem unfolds between them, ultimately served as disempowering in some ways as it rendered her a bad scientist.[25] Laroche's provocative piece on carrots-as-dildos in *The Merry Wives of Windsor* underscores how a connection between women and the vegetable kingdom might be understood as empowering – even quite literally pleasurable.[26] The essay we penned together for *Shakespeare Studies* brings together food studies and ecofeminism to rethink the Queen's role in the garden scene in *Richard II*, such that it is the queen, and not Richard, whose connection to earth, to the herb rue, is tragically underappreciated.[27] And Munroe's more recent piece, 'Is it Really Ecocritical If it isn't Feminist?', in its reading of *Titus Andronicus*, argues for the imperative to do work that combines the ecological and the feminist:

> If ecocriticism does not take the work of materialist feminists and ecofeminists seriously, especially the discussion of lived, real power relations and practices (even as we are aware that these practices come to us by way of representation), it might talk a good talk about how we are all 'matter', but in so doing, it risks reifying the very binary it aims to deconstruct.[28]

Although work that declares itself ecofeminist is to date still relatively scarce in early modern studies, we might turn to other early modern and Shakespeare scholarship that is implicitly ecofeminist in its approach to help us begin to understand the potential for ecofeminist work in this period. Louise Noble's recent work on Aemilia Lanyer elaborates on how Lanyer's anthropomorphizing of nonhuman nature, and the alignment of women with it, 'produces a poetics of ecological awareness deeply critical of existing hierarchical systems that exploit both people and the environment'.[29] A growing corpus of work related to household cookery and medicine, even if not 'ecofeminist' as such, is very much in line with the sort of ecofeminist theory we lay out here. Hillary Nunn's piece on greensickness, 'On Vegetating Virgins', looks to the link between women and vegetation in illustrations of greensick women (and the way the disease ostensibly threatened to move them closer to the denigrated vegetable realm) to rethink how 'precariously greensick women cling to the edges of the human'.[30]

Such work on cooking and medicine illustrates how ecofeminist principles, even if not also ecofeminist vocabulary, might be applied to ask new questions of materials that are both new and old to us. By revisiting different aspects of women's material practice, including but not necessarily only household work (which is often gendered in more complicated ways, too) – the objects with which women interact on a daily basis in the home, the garden, the fields, the streets, the theatre, the church – we might find alternative expressions of human–nonhuman relations that are informed by gender as well as by race and class. Such expressions may not be written, or at least we may well look beyond print sources; they may be in manuscript, or visual, or we may attend to the objects themselves, the mundane 'things' that punctuate the sort of 'affordances' that we discuss later in Chapters 1 and 4.

Early modern women's medicine and cookery provides one example of the vibrancy of women's material practices, which simultaneously illuminates a multifaceted ecological and social history; women's domestic work expresses a relationship with the nonhuman world enmeshed with complex and contradictory social power relations, which their daily practices both resisted and reinforced. As we discuss more at length in individual chapters in this book, the way women cultivated, used and understood the plants, animals and minerals featured in their home remedies and cookery provides information about their day-to-day activities as well as how those activities were shaped by women's particular social and historical circumstances. Attending to the implications of, say, particular differences in the way plants and animals figured in women's household cookery and medicine versus the same earthly creatures in scientific experiments by Royal Society members yields readings of these ingredients, Fellows and meanings that depend on the specifically 'social' as well as the 'ecological'.

1

Ecofeminism matters

[T]he human is always the very stuff of the messy, contingent, emergent mix of the material world.[1]

In the chapters that follow in this book, we demonstrate how an application of some of the principles of ecofeminist theory we have discussed in the Introduction allows us to reorient and defamiliarize categories of enquiry that have thus far been of import to Shakespeare studies – in particular, 'the Domestic', 'Knowledge-Making' and 'Subject–Object Relations'. Each of these has been the topic in recent decades of ecocritical/feminist scholarship, but ecofeminist theory gives us the opportunity to consider them anew and to think about how the concerns of ecological and feminist theorists might be brought into dialogue to help us understand the interconnected relations between them. What is more, within an ecofeminist discussion, the boundaries of these discursive topics begin to dissolve, finding space in which the domestic concerns merge with knowledge-making, and both disrupt the relationship between subject and object. In this dissolution, we can start to see the continuity and disjuncture between early modern ways of being and thinking and our own.

Domesticated beings

Using ecofeminist theory, we look to interrupt the 'natural' woman–nature alliance associated with the domestic sphere by combining readings of Shakespeare with household texts associated with and owned by women, as these books usefully reveal a relationship not always in alignment with but rather sometimes antagonistic to the natural world.[2] They disclose women's roles in maintaining the illusion of control over nature, as moth holes in clothing and mice droppings in the flour would defy that control. Thus the 'domestic' as a category, as discussed by so many feminists in a variety of insightful ways, is a subject that also has profound ecological implications.

At its root, the domestic implies a set of binaries – inside/outside, culture/nature, human/nonhuman, clean/dirty, cooked/raw – detrimental to ecological thinking around what belongs within the house and what belongs without its walls. 'The domestic' is also a heavily gendered domain, as a space that is associated with the female, particularly from its Victorian 'angel in the house' constructions. As a result, it has been widely considered by feminist theorists and critics, but it has not been a category regarded at any length by ecocritics, perhaps because in its very construction it assumes an exclusion of 'the natural'. While feminist critics of early modernity such as Wendy Wall have explored the anxiety around demonic potentials in women's actual domestic work of medicine making and meal preparing, ecofeminism interrogates the very real boundaries maintained in deference to the domestic delusion of exclusion and the othering of the nonhuman.[3] In confronting the presence of pest control in particular in domestic discourse, we proceed to deconstruct one of its primal oppositions (cat and mouse) with Shakespearean examples and ecofeminist tools. From there, we move to the spider, moth, fly and the like to show how the movement of these 'lesser creatures' across household boundaries exposes not only literal holes that might be exploited, but also the fundamental delusion of containment. And finally, we move to fire, that which is necessary in the home but also destructive if it leaps its bounds, as a way of reconceptualizing domestic tasks within a larger ecological framework.

While plays like Shakespeare's *The Taming of the Shrew* have served as material to explore anxieties related to women's place in marriage, the household and domestic economies, as Natasha Korda and others have pointed out, women's work itself remains, still today, largely 'invisible';[4] ecofeminism's project, like theirs, is fundamentally recuperative, and brings to the fore women's work, their material and practical lives. Ecofeminism, with its particular emphasis on the 'socio-ecological', troubles the category of the domestic to consider how an interrogation of women's household labour in the context of a combined feminist and ecological approach traverses multiple boundaries, how the household itself is a marker for the illusion (and delusion) of containment – of space, of bodies, of gendered identity, of nonhuman creatures and non-living things. That is, ecofeminist theory offers a rethink premised on the notion of 'transcorporeality'; if, as Stacy Alaimo posits, the human self and the environment that self occupies are both jointly the products (and co-producers) of one another, then the notion of discrete boundaries, that a 'thing' (or person-as-thing) might be contained, is in fact an impossibility.[5] Early modern scholars have considered such 'ecological' premises of ontological co-creation, but their interest has tended to consider the household more as generic, not gendered space.[6] In the interest of recuperating a richer and more multi-dimensional sense of human–nonhuman relations, though, we need to think of containment fantasies related to the household in terms of the multiple forms of subjection that we discussed in the Introduction. Without suggesting that Shakespeare was somehow aware of this idea, we propose here that some of Shakespeare's works anticipate what this application of ecofeminism has more recently been able to articulate; the works we discuss demonstrate how anxieties about women's containment were inextricably linked to those about the subjection of nonhuman things, the potentially invasive forces and materials – mice, fire, moths, wind and others – that threatened the seeming boundaries established to protect the men and women that inhabited the house and its environs.

Ecofeminist theory, in its joint interest in both the social and the ecological, forces us to reassess how material is inextricably linked to material practices and how co-agentic material processes are intertwined with the material power relations that asserted, but could never truly establish, women's containment within the house. Instead of boundedness, women's work reveals a fundamental 'embeddedness' in which humans and nonhumans are fundamentally entangled.[7] In so asserting, we draw on how Korda proposes the household to be a site of 'multiple exchanges', economic and human, that reveal the permeable boundaries between inside and outside rather than their discreet and manageable borders.[8] And to her materialist feminist reconceptualization, we add the ecological: these 'exchanges' simultaneously serve as co-productive happenings that alter the qualities of the human and nonhuman things in question such that the lines between human and nonhuman, cook and fire, patient and cordial, are not simply transgressed but prove to be a fundamental human delusion. As such, we revisit the way early modern scholars have discussed the chaotic nature of households, as Wall does in *Staging Domesticity*, when she writes, 'Representations of domestic disorder on the stage might thus simply be said to anatomize the wayward passions to be mastered or pathologies to be cured so as to ensure the proper ordering of home and polity',[9] and begin to think of the impulses to manipulate diet, to manage flesh, to defy mortality (through preservation of food or people) as fruitless efforts not because they were simply unachieved by all housewives, but rather because these efforts reflected that such management was an impossibility all along.[10]

Attempted acts of enclosure, whether of the garden, the (especially female) body, the pantry or the house, betray how the impulse to subject one force or body to another is futile. It is an illusion not simply because the household was a chaotic more than an ordered space, but instead, as ecofeminist theory helps us articulate, what we call 'chaos' in this context is not antithetical to order but is the very quality of co-agentic human and nonhuman materials that defy control, which is the aim of enclosure. For example, the rosemary, angelica and rosewater in a fortifying plague water serve to do more than just order the human body (humoral or otherwise) through the absorption of plant material into human stomach, blood and cell tissue. To say as much would be to reassert the boundary between human and plant, even if one is incorporated into another, and it reinscribes the notion of human agency over plant (as human ingests, human body absorbs the passive plant object). Rather, ecofeminist theory helps orient us to the exchange between plant and human body that defies order or easy categorization, causing us to reassess the process of ingestion and absorption as simultaneous instances of plant/human 'intraconnection' and 'entanglement'.[11] These materials, human and nonhuman alike, collaborate such that what we want to call the human itself is a composite, not a distinct thing, and so too the nonhuman as well.

Ecofeminist theory, moreover, also asks us to revisit the social and historical implications of such a reassessment. It is, for instance, not an unimportant detail that anxieties about household order went hand in hand with anxieties about managing the housewife – her body, her behaviour, her passions – and we see this in particular with the discourse around kitchen fires in the period. Domestic cookery and medicine were areas of early modern life that used ingredients and processes that are co-creative with their would-be human agents, but they also served to reinforce ideas about women's containment within the house, that household work was women's domain, burgeoning conceptions that served as the contested context for second-wave feminism. Ecofeminism helps us redefine the binaries wild/domestic, inside/outside household, women/men, housework/professional work, nonhuman/human – and so, 'domesticated' comes to refer to a bevvy of human and nonhuman things in the context of containment. Ecofeminism emphasizes how both the containment of seemingly subjected humans and of nonhuman beings, and their linked qualities, are imagined more than realized states of being.

On the other side of the question of containment, however, is the intimacy that arises from the material practices historically linked with the household. In growing, preserving and, yes, even domesticating animals and plants, humans come to know them in their diurnal and seasonal cycles. In this revaluation of these ways of knowing and in this other definition of 'domestic' as the familiar, therefore, ecofeminist enquiry returns us again to a sense of embeddedness, of shared susceptibilities and co-creative exchanges.

Knowing things

Even as ideas about the household, which might be contained within and defined as domestic, were in flux in this period, so too were ways of valuing knowledge; and new ways of knowing nonhuman things went hand-in-hand with human subjection of 'Nature'. But what does it mean to know something, to know a *thing*? Whose knowledge counts? We have inherited a Cartesian value system that recognizes rationality (with its related term, cognition) as the foundation of knowledge, but what if efforts 'to know' something simply betrays the limits of cognition? And what if things themselves might *know*, might have an existence beyond our human knowing? Vital materialist and posthumanist scholarship have ventured into this territory, aiming to reorient our understanding of things, of knowledge. Jane Bennett's now-familiar rat, glove, bottle cap, stick, pollen tableau observes 'stuff that commanded attention in its own right, as existents in excess of their association with human meanings, habits, or projects' and points to the 'vibrant agency' of things.[12] Even Francis

Bacon, who insisted on the primacy of human reason and rationality over the senses, which 'deceive', also acknowledges that as 'interpreter of Nature', Man has limits; Man may be the 'interpreter of Nature', but he is also Nature's 'servant'.[13] How, though, might such 'existents in excess' that Bennett proposes be recognized but through a human lens? After all, such things may have agency beyond human signification, but we are asked to think about them anew as assemblages apprehended, comprehended, by humans and within a context that is as much cultural as 'natural'. Bennett rightly asks us to consider the 'dangerous' agency of things, that which 'will always exceed our knowledge and control', as in her example of electricity and ours of fire, but it is ultimately we humans who articulate that excess, that danger, not nonhuman things themselves.[14]

While posthumanist work like Bennett's challenges our conception of how 'things' themselves might be agents, we need still to deconstruct the 'us', the 'human' to which she refers, as it potentially reifies the 'Man' Bacon understood as the legitimized knower, the primary apprehender and interlocutor of things. That is, until we dismantle the seemingly universal 'human' of 'human meanings', then the 'we', that 'us', the 'human', becomes yet another substitute for dominant ideas and perspectives. What if, that is, instead of the question of whether or not nonhuman 'things' also have agency, we concentrate on the interstitial territory between what appears to be within the realm of human apprehension and that which exceeds it, the elusive qualities rather than universalizing potential of meaning? What if we ask not what else we might know about nonhuman things but rather what it is that exceeds the limits of what we might know and how it has been tied culturally and historically to anxieties about the excess of Others? What if we look to different ways of knowing altogether, those that simultaneously redress the limits of the category 'human' and the 'denial of ecological embeddedness', to use Val Plumwood's language, by making central that which defies human control and not the attempts to control themselves, at the same time we elucidate the fallacy of the collective human 'we'?[15]

Ecofeminist theory provides a framework to interrogate the ontological co-evolution of things, human and nonhuman alike, such that we can embrace the 'ecological embeddedness' Plumwood describes; yet it simultaneously explicates how the multiplicity of the 'we', of the 'human' is experienced in diverse ways – raced, classed and gendered. To revalue embedded experience is also to revalue this (bio)diversity and chaotic multiplicity, the limits of the 'human' in ways that relate to environmental justice concerns and to reconstitute frameworks of knowledge whereby we also value wonder, the unknown or not-yet-known.[16] In so doing, ecofeminists may simultaneously intervene in networks that privilege reason and objectivity over embodiment and experiential knowledge and those that subjugate racial Others, the poor, women and nonhuman beings – in particular, networks of scientific knowledge that became formally established in early modern England and that still dominate today.

Where once Fate or a divine/supernatural agent controlled the mysterious workings of 'nature' that eluded human apprehension, early modern science increasingly posited a new, distinctively earthly agent of knowledge: the objective natural philosopher. Such objectivity required by definition a distancing of the object to be known from the knower, the subject; and, as many have discussed, this distancing was a simultaneously gendered act, where women were increasingly partitioned into the category of object/known, men the subject/knower. In this growing area of the philosophy of 'nature', as Val Plumwood writes, both women and the nonhuman became stripped of their agentic qualities, the objects of the investigative gaze of male scientists: 'In the subject/object division the "object" is treated as passive, the one acted upon, and the knower is the active party who forces knowledge from the reluctant or mute object.'[17] What changed, that is, was not so much that a dominant, masculine agent (a divine or the male scientist) occupied the subject role, women and nonhuman things the object role, but whether the subject–object relationship existed in what we might call first a supernatural, later a 'natural' framework. Ecofeminist theory might help us reimagine possible new frameworks that lead us beyond the divide that the supernatural-to-natural shift might suggest.

What Donna Haraway deems the 'so far', the embracing of what is not yet known, may be key to how ecofeminist theory can help us think outside of such binary systems.[18] With this in mind, we emphasize here a third category, neither strictly natural nor supernatural, but something else, a category of wonder, of what we do not yet know and possibly will never know. We are not, of course, the first to draw on this idea, nor are we the first to suggest its relation to early modern history or Shakespeare and are in part motivated by the possible dialogue between an ecofeminist approach and the recent analyses of Loraine Daston and Mary Floyd-Wilson, who use the word 'preternatural' for this category.[19] However, we want to invoke in this third category not just an alternative way of knowing related both to early modern science and relevant to ecostudies, but rather to articulate a particularly ecofeminist understanding of the epoch of knowledge-making practices and technologies dubbed the Anthropocene. By doing so, following Haraway in her discussion of the Chthulucene, we aim to disrupt both the anthropocentrism inherent to such a characterization as well as the androcentrism that the Anthropocene might be said to reify; ecofeminist theory offers an alternative to what has become orthodoxy within ecological scholarship, especially its nearly ubiquitous framing around the Anthropocene, which is possible only when we 'destabilize worlds of thinking with other worlds of thinking'.[20] These 'other worlds of thinking' are found, Haraway argues, by reorienting the frameworks within and from which we understand the world we inhabit such that we emphasize a knowledge based on 'endosymbiotic' relationships between all things, human and nonhuman alike, a web of interconnected multiple somethings rather than bounded individual beings

– a sort of 'ecological embeddedness'. While posthumanism addresses similar questions, an ecofeminist approach specifically negates – along with the individualism intrinsic to dominant modern science – the notion of a divide between subject and object that is at the heart of race, class and gender inequality and so often justified by science.

Ecofeminism pushes us beyond the either-or of trying to align Shakespeare's writings with a particular approach to knowledge and consider its implications for human–nonhuman relationships, as may interest ecocritics, or of aiming to position Shakespeare's ideas within a particular set of discourses about knowledge that may or may not afford women agency, as feminist scholars might prioritize. In doing so, ecofeminist theory might help us stop asking who 'knows' what (and who is prohibited from knowing), which tethers us to the subject/object binary, to ask how agency might be available to both nonhumans and women as well as the poor and otherwise subjugated (and how they are linked in practical and representational contexts) by way of their association with the unknown or even the unknowable.

A substance of subject–objects

As is apparent above, subject–object relations fundamental to discourses about knowledge-making in early modern England were also at the centre of thinking about new ways to experience what we now term subjectivity. And subjectivity, ground well explored within early modern studies, is a topic that ecofeminist theory can help us revisit in useful ways. The now-familiar notion of 'self-fashioning' predicated on a tension between self and social forces emphasizes how identity, whether individual or collective, is dependent on expressly human agents. Feminist and gender studies in early modern studies have pushed us to rethink how such 'self-fashioning' might have its limitations, as definitions of a 'self', or subject, are premised on biology or representative of dominant (white, male) groups. Still, this work for the most part retains its focus on the human, on the give-and-take of subjectivity dependent on a spectrum of individual will and social forces, even if the influence of each has shifted over time in our scholarly discourse. We have found different ways to ask, for example, about the extent to which Desdemona can possibly fashion herself as innocent when Iago, even Othello, have determined her to be otherwise; or to ponder how the idealizing narrative of the lover–beloved relationship in the sonnets is predicated on an intrinsic misogyny. When we do so, though, and much productive work has come from doing so, we nevertheless understand subjectivity and gendered identity based exclusively on human relationships, where examples of the nonhuman tend to serve as metaphoric gestures more than the material objects themselves.

Scholars have turned recently to thinking about subjectivity as connected to the physical environments – including our bodies – that we inhabit; such approaches usefully move away from anthropocentrism to include nonhumans as well as humans. As Mary Floyd-Wilson and Garrett Sullivan remind us, 'in early modern thinking, transactions between body and environment usually imply a conception of subjectivity or social identity'.[21] For Floyd-Wilson and Sullivan, not all such 'transactions' necessarily involve a wilful subject or are based in cognition (as in the case of respiration), but 'a majority of transactions between body and environment in this period seem to presuppose the subject; either subjectivity emerges through these transactions, or the subject seems to shape their nature, or both'.[22] While this transactional way of thinking about subjectivity shaped by the relationship between self and inhabited environment moves us away from anthropocentric ways of thinking to some extent, it retains a sense of a divided, even if collaborative, (human) subject and (nonhuman) object. Practitioners of new materialism have challenged this divide and urged us to reconsider how (human) self/subject and (nonhuman) Other/object might be co-constructed such that what appears to be a discrete (human) individual is really an ontological composite of human and nonhuman agents. In arguing for a political ecology of 'things' with 'power', for instance, Jane Bennett emphasizes the co-agential quality of humans and, say, electrical grid or carrot.[23] Stacy Alaimo's work on 'transcorporeality' also foregrounds the co-agential quality of things, blurring the lines between what we tend to think of as (human) subject and (nonhuman) object such that they are embedded, ontologically co-created 'things', the boundaries between one and the other inscrutable.[24]

These approaches take as their matter, albeit in different ways, a subject–object relationship, whether that subject is discretely human or is human and nonhuman combined in such a way that the subject and object blend indiscriminately. In Chapter 4, we draw on how ecofeminism helps us reconceptualize how the subject–object relationship, upon which human subjectivity is founded, is simultaneously grounded in the multiple forms of subjection discussed in the Introduction. That is, with an emphasis on the 'socio-ecological' transactional qualities of self/Other, human/nonhuman, male/female, human/nonhuman, rich/poor, colonizer/colonized, binaries that ecofeminism might help us usefully interrogate, ecofeminist theory might also bring us to understand subjectivity differently.

Ecofeminist theory's emphasis on multi-dimensional context, on the transactionality of the social and the ecological together, can help us read Shakespeare's work and conceive of gendered subjectivity in the period anew. To do so, we push back against much posthumanism, which wants to marginalize human contact while not able fully to absent the perceiver who is doing the analysis.[25] We might recall how Bennett's tableau of debris described at the beginning of *Vibrant Matter* relegates the inner-city context of which these things are a part to the outskirts of her analysis.[26] Such marginalization of context is particularly problematic given the location of the Baltimore protests of 2015, for instance, and recurrent social crises may indeed make us confront the fact that many of these theories, at their origins, begin by placing social issues in parentheses. The dominant-reifying potential of divorcing such context is evident in Ian Bogost's response to the question of 'what it's like to be a thing' in *Alien Phenomenology*, in which he makes a statement that only an English-speaking white man can – 'Today, most would accept that British men are no more intrinsically worthy than women, Congalese, horses, and redwoods' – as if all it takes is a white man's say-so to relegate misogyny, racism, animal abuse and ecological devastation to the past.[27] In seeking to articulate the vibrancy of things, it would thus seem, women or Congolese or redwood become the 'fixed' categories – as both ameliorated and unchanging, and thus no longer requiring our attention. Recognizing that Bogost would believe this assessment to miss the point – that his theory is 'not about that' – we assert that this is *precisely* the point: a more comprehensive awareness of ecological devastation shows how all kinds of denigration are linked. If ecocriticism embraces these theories without an eye to gender, race or class, it loses sight of the real sociological implications of the endeavour. What is happening/what has happened to the earth is happening/has happened to all of us (human and nonhuman, men and women, Norwegian and African, polar bear and honeybee), but not equally.

In search of an alternative, we turn to the work of Harry Heft, who, in response to James Gibson's brand of ecological psychology, argues for the 'dynamic quality' of perceptual experience, in which the object does not just have vitality, as Bennett would have it, but it also lives in vital relation to its context, one partially shared with the perceiver. An ecofeminist application of what Heft calls 'affordances' is a potentially useful way to reconceptualize how such entangled transactions work in everyday practice. As Heft proposes, cognition itself is shaped by perception, by 'affordances' – or the means by which we experience our relationship to 'things' that is at once intellectual, tactile and corporeal. The environments with which we inhabit 'are perceived in the course of action; they are a part of a flow of activity and awareness'.[28]

Thus, within the concept of affordances 'there is a blurred line between subject and object by way of activity with/in an environment (where one stops and the other starts is murky)' and 'subject–object relations, and subjectivity, are not defined by cognition but rather activity across/within different boundaries (body, home, environs, etc); they are perceptual rather than conceptual'.[29] This may sound a lot like phenomenological figurations, but the world of affordances is also a world of values, of 'oughts', as Heft writes, and there is much to gain by thinking through how the environment–embodiment relationship is 'valued' in gendered terms.[30] Understanding such 'transactions' in terms of a perceptual relationship of the sort 'affordances' detail, but historically and culturally contextualized to account for differential race, class and/or gender experience, may help us understand subjectivity itself in new ways. As a result, an ecofeminist reading engages 'dynamism' over 'vibrancy', and in doing so acknowledges the subject position of either the observer/theorist or the one who does the knowing as part of this dynamism.

Ecofeminist theory asks us to put pressure on both these perceptual transactions: what constitutes them, the way they challenge the boundary between body and environment, and their implications for understanding gendered subjectivity. By understanding these multispecies encounters as not dependent on will, or even cognition, we might reimagine their implications for subjectivity no longer to necessitate volition but to be mutually contingent upon multiple social and ecological forces and things; as such, human body (previously subject) and nonhuman environment (previously object) merge such that they are a subject–object, neither distinguishable from the other. Moreover, since such transactions are contextual, situated within matrices of power for which 'subject' is, say, default white male, and female or colonial subjectivity is inherently Other, ecofeminism's link between the social and the ecological is of particular import to changing how our interpretation of these transactions must necessarily take into consideration race, class and/or gender.

In Chapter 4 we consider how the traces of such transactional relationships found in Shakespeare's works foreground the interplay between humans and nonhumans in such a way that draws on the sort of valuing that 'affordances' articulate. Our ecofeminist reading of these works demonstrates how Shakespeare at times challenges notions of gendered subjectivity predicated on (human/male) subject and (nonhuman/female) object such that these very distinctions, and their socially constructed value systems, disintegrate. With a focus on historically contextualized material practice, we consider attempts to position both women and nonhumans as objects (particularly for us here, plants) against which the (male) subject's identity might be constituted in Shakespeare's works; but instead of discrete boundaries, of a distinct self and Other, subjects and objects collide, interact, transact, envelop, make and remake one another, revealing only the elusive traces of boundaries between them. As Heft's analysis reminds us, though, the 'dynamic quality' of the subject–objects in question may be inherently co-created 'things', but 'things' themselves exist within historically contingent contexts that include value systems. Lived experience of/as things, that is, happens within power systems where gender matters too.

For a specific example, we consider how plants in the early modern period have an integral function within the realm of medicine; thus the analysis of their appearances in the period should be instilled with the threat of disease and the promise of potential cure. While these aspects have much to do with human concerns, they also have much to do with the history of their propagation (by which we do not necessarily assume human cultivation) and their place in local environments. To ignore this context because such a focus would highlight qualities that appeal to humans is to disregard much of the agentic force that plants may have.[31] That the early moderns held this valuing as equal to any aesthetic merits (the kitchen garden stood alongside the pleasure garden) is an essential aspect of understanding botanical agency in the period, one that mitigates surface-level readings of beautiful, love-denoting flowers.[32] By returning to the historical context, we may better comprehend how biochemical 'advancements' may have dissipated some of that agentic potential and exacerbated our ecological crisis. That is, if we were more dependent on living things for the maintenance of our health, we might be more careful with the places they grow. What is more, through the historical foil, we may see how the displacement of food sources from consumers absents the labour of cultivation and harvesting from the thing itself, reducing a being that takes months to seed, bloom and ripen to a surface-level, consumer-ready object. Shakespeare's plays and poems, along with the texts that capture material practices of the period, such as gardening manuals, books of secrets and recipe books, point us directly to an historical dynamism and interdependency that destabilizes an unreflective consumerist mentality. What is more, in these writings, we are able to see how material practice interrupts gender and human/nonhuman binaries that reify difference without acknowledging shared susceptibilities.

Historical practice and present crisis

We conclude this chapter with two instances that prompt the reading practices that ecofeminism wants to instigate in readers of Shakespeare. Each engages all of the above topics – the transcorporeal domestic, knowledge-making and subject–object relations. One from the early seventeenth century comes from a recipe book owned by Lady Frances Catchmay and compiled around 1625. The other is an account of the Zika crisis happening today. This move from archival digging to presentist application reflects that of each of the following chapters, because throughout this study we try to step outside our historically rooted analyses to consider immediate resonances and applications. These initial examples help us to explore the essential interplay in ecofeminist work between historical precedent and current crises.

A recipe from Lady Catchmay's manuscript receipt book serves as a reminder of how the three subjects that are the topic of the main chapters of this book overlap, how they are inherently themselves transactional categories. As Korda reminds us, the household was defined 'as much by objects as it was by subjects'.[33] Households were also sites of multiple thresholds crossed over and over again – the doorway, the mouth, the ear, the garden wall – by multiple creatures and substances, human and nonhuman alike. These 'exchanges', as Korda details, function as reminders of the fluidity of things; but they also recall, as we argue throughout this book, the collaborative relations that comprise them. In an entry for stopping a nosebleed from Catchmay's book, we find the following pithy cure: 'Take alittle fine peece of linen clothe and aspider kill him not, but winde him in the peace of clothe, and put it vpp in the nostrells of the patient and the bloud shall stopp; by gods grace proved.'[34] At the centre sits a live spider, the spectre of the household pest, elsewhere the thing to be eradicated from within domestic enclosures. Here, nonhuman material that has already mingled with the human – the linen cloth manufactured from plant material – mingles yet again with animal and human, as the spider is wrapped in the cloth, then placed inside the patient's nasal passage.[35] Human blood and tissue combine with cloth and spider to stop the nosebleed. While it may be tempting to assume that the bleeding ceases because of the nose obstruction, there is likely more to it than that. Spider webs have long been known to speed coagulation, so it may well be that this cure works because the spider inside the cloth produces fresh webbing that mixes with blood and cell tissue inside the nostrils to do so; the antiseptic and antifungal properties of the web, itself produced of the amino acids that were the result of another transactional relationship within and across the spider's body, traverses the threshold that seemingly demarcates human and nonhuman boundaries to reveal instead an intensive collaboration between them. The line between (human) subject and (nonhuman) object blurs, becoming unrecognizable, unintelligible, ultimately *unknowable*. That examples like this stem from household work, a decidedly gendered area of early modern life, makes them of particular import to reading Shakespeare and inhabits the multiple categories of our analysis in the ways that ecofeminist theory may inform them anew.

In the chapters that follow, we use ecofeminist theory alongside readings of Shakespeare's work to rethink these categories. We might position the moment when Marcus Andronicus exhibits no compassion when a fly disturbs the room alongside his and others' outrage when his niece – the 'deer/dear' of Titus's description – is raped and mutilated in order to think about how the play reflects on the intimate bonds between human and nonhuman. Or how such intimacy appears in *King Lear* as a reminder of how the thresholds we believe separate us from nonhumans, even from the weather, are themselves an illusion. That medicine and cookery, understood as domains of women, expresses these vulnerabilities, these delusions, makes it an area that pairs especially well with ecofeminist readings of Shakespeare.

It may seem a far stretch from an ailment as common as a nosebleed to the Zika virus, which in pregnant women has been connected with microcephaly in infants. Much of the perceived disparity blooms from the global sense of scale afforded by mass media, pandemic and the World Health Organization. When examined closely, however, representations of the Zika crisis reflect similar issues about gendered permeable bodies, the transactional relations between human and nonhuman, self and Other, and the sphere of the unknown/unknowable. Our example here is a *Guardian* article from 11 February 2016.

Immediately after the title of the article, 'Climate Change may have helped spread Zika virus, according to WHO scientists', the reader is confronted with the image that would seem to encapsulate the crisis: a young woman with dark skin, clad in a bikini top with perceptibly pregnant belly exposed, stands in a dirty street of an obviously impoverished area with pools of water behind her. The caption reads 'Tamires da Costa, 16, who is four months pregnant, stands in a street with standing flood water next to her home in the Parque Sao Bento shantytown of Rio de Janeiro'.[36] The juxtaposition of title and image immediately establishes the impact of the environment on raced, classed and gendered bodies to be anatomized in the article. Zika itself, sexually transmitted and mildly flu-like, only establishes its crisis status through the womb, that dark space of maternal protection becoming a nightmare of deformity. In speaking of sociological implications of the disease, moreover, scientists begin to reproduce this womb-space into metaphor. Biologist Daniel Brooks declares:

> This is likely to become an equal opportunity crisis ... The developing, poorer countries are impacted disproportionately but they deal with these diseases all the time, they are not surprised by them. But in Europe and North America, people have lived in a bubble where we think our wealth and technology can protect us from climate change. And that's not true.[37]

As if tragically severed from the feminized protective space, developed countries find themselves vulnerable. Climate change becomes enacted in perceivable ways on the bodies of the rich as well as the poor. In attempts to mitigate this impact, the response has been ultrasound technology that can know this impact before delivery, technology which is not as readily available to the poor as the rich.

If we look closer, however, the permeability of human bodies with the environment is not just relegated to the female of the species, as the disease is spread by the non-discriminating mosquito. Within the *Guardian* web-article sits an embedded link: a man in a black uniform holds a bazooka-sized pesticide gun, waist high, below him the words 'Should we wipe mosquitoes off the face of the earth?'[38] The article, which discusses the debate among scientists about 'editing nature', about whether or not it is in human interest to develop a genetic modification within the Aedes aegypti mosquito that carries the disease, begins in pointedly gendered terms: 'When an Aedes aegypti mosquito bites you, she – because only the females, which need blood as nutrients for their offspring, bite – will probe your skin with her proboscis as many as 20 times.'[39] This statement undoes the image of the vulnerable teenage body within the frame article, such that the female of the mosquito species recalls James Cameron's alien creature, deadly protector of her young. All human bodies are susceptible to her probing, threatening not only female wombs but also male seed. In the act of puncturing, mosquito, virus, blood and human are united.

The article goes on to structure the debate in binary terms, terms that may emotionally obfuscate the real issue: human overconsumption, not only of fossil fuels but also of plastics, which offer 'the mosquitos ... an ideal breeding ground'. It turns out that the large standing pools of flood water in dirt streets menacing the perceptibly pregnant girl are not where the 'real danger' lies. The journalist Archie Bland concludes with insight:

> there is a certain bitter irony that in an attempt to beat a disease whose impact will be felt most keenly by women and their unborn children, and which has been exacerbated by a shortage of funding for studies that would focus on the wellbeing of women in developing countries, we are contemplating a macho solution that entails sending male mosquitoes to impregnate as many females as possible, with the ultimate ambition of wiping the enemy off the face of the Earth.[40]

Within the writing of the piece, the pesticide bazooka from the thumbnail becomes a figure for the 'macho' science that eradicates the Other (gendered female) rather than modify consumerist practice. Masculinized technological innovation trumps feminized womb-space/threatening and violent female creatures who defy its passive constraints.

This image may similarly stand against the work of this study. Rather than inhabit a poisonous fog that only exacerbates our current crisis, the analysis that follows requires a certain clarity as well as an appreciation of irony. It asks us to see ourselves as both the source and the solution, and to seek out in the language of the past, the seeds of present paradigms and future blossoming. In doing so, it does not idealize the language or the practice of the past, but rather sees in the past a destabilizing potential in this unthinking world.

2

Of mouseholes and housefires: Transcorporeal domesticity

And this the cranny is, right and sinister ...[1]

You must ... know that when you lay your séedes in the ground, they are like so many good men amongst a world of wicked ones, and as it were inuironed and begirt with manie Armies of enemies ...[2]

We can no longer retain the comfortable human-centred illusion of separate casts of characters in separate dramas.[3]

Climate is not just for polar bears any more. Nor is it felt only by vulnerable developing sea-level nations, though they still bear the brunt of its present and future calamity. Not only are many regions of the world feeling the effects of extreme weather, but the furious fossil fuel extraction assumed under the looming threat of regulation has also impacted diverse communities across the globe. As with Little Red Riding Hood, the wolf is not elsewhere, but in the house wearing your grandmother's clothes, and environmental catastrophe is not just something that is happening in the Arctic, but it can be as immediate as flames, or tainted water, coming out of your kitchen tap. As our gazes move from the frozen frontiers of human habitation to more recognizable, domestic spaces, ecofeminist enquiry becomes most relevant. It is the very permeability of the boundaries between domestic concerns and wild frontiers, moreover, that becomes the object of that enquiry.

Shakespeare helps us to understand this permeable relationship between the wild and the domestic in the way that his characters move between 'green worlds' and cultured spaces yet the space representing both – the stage – remains the same. Illustrating this non-divide is the moment when Puck raises spectres in chasing the Mechanicals from the forest; the phantasms are not all inherently frightening, though, not all necessarily *of the forest*:

> I'll follow you, I'll lead you about a round!
> Through bog, through bush, through brake, through brier;
> Sometime a horse I'll be, sometime a hound,
> A hog, a headless bear, sometime a fire;
> And neigh, and bark, and grunt, and roar, and burn,
> Like horse, hound, hog, bear, fire, at every turn.
> (*MND* 3.1.100–5)

The hog, hound, horse and fire have domestic associations, but in this context, the implication is that they have been 'unleashed' and are running wild, making them frightening because they are uncontained in the forest; it is their place relative to domestic enclosures, not their intrinsic qualities, that determines their status as wild or tame. Granted, their tragic potential remains controlled because Puck's phantasms are just that unreal, but incidents of wild fires and being chased by ferocious beasts haunt the Shakespearean audience as frightening possibilities, as the recorded vigilance against household fires and the many recipes for 'biting of a mad dog' attest. For the early moderns, house fires and mad dogs are not forest encounters; they are experienced in the context of the everyday. The fear that Puck invokes here is not of the wild as such, but the untamed as it is potentially located within domesticated spaces, at once a destroyer of the illusion of safety as well as a threat in itself. They are made more frightening, more haunting, because the hearth and loyal dog are at the core of what was deemed most safe – the home.

This chapter presents the domestic structures signifying the home and their penetrability as a means of exposing the inherently illusory quality of the very boundaries the category of the 'domestic' appears to demarcate, or, as Val Plumwood writes, 'the idea that human life takes place in a self-enclosed, completely humanized and cultural space that is somehow independent of an inessential sphere of nature which exists in a remote space "somewhere else"'.[4] No matter how rich and seemingly impervious the households, such as those of Pyramus' and Thisbe's Babylonian parents, fissures inevitably appear in the surrounding walls. While exterior walls were meant to protect the home and its environs from enemy invaders (from such human enemies as the Montagues in *Romeo and Juliet* to the rabbits or livestock that might ravage the enclosed garden spaces such walls surround), house walls kept out the elements and creeping creatures – but only to some extent. Some beings nevertheless make their way into the house from the outside, as seen in Gower's invocation of homespun night-time in *Pericles*, for instance, 'The cat, with eyne of burning coal, / Now couches 'fore the mouse's hole; /And crickets at the oven's mouth / Sing the blither for their drouth' (3.Ch.5–8). Some, like the cat and the oven fire (importantly not lit here), are invited; others, the mouse and cricket, make their way in by other means. The fact that the passage continues, 'Hymen hath brought the bride to bed, / Where by the loss of maidenhead / A babe is moulded' (3.Ch.9–11), shows just how this porousness of indoor spaces is completely entangled with figurations of penetrable female bodies. As feminist critiques have done much to dismantle walls in examining the intact hymen/enclosed garden that represents the virginal female body throughout the Christian literary tradition by interjecting female will and voice, an ecofeminist reading returns to the material walls of the environment and considers their roles in maintaining this illusion of enclosed human – particularly domestic – spaces. These material barriers stand against the encroachment of nature/the wild/the nonhuman and thus become literal manifestations of binary structures that pit domesticated against untamed, binaries that also have much to do with female bodies and their regulation.

Through an examination of nonhuman things in and around Shakespeare's texts – here, small creatures and fire, both of which exist within and without domestic spaces – we expose the failings in these walls. In exposing these susceptibilities we simultaneously uncover the delusion that buttresses them and confront fear at its source. Ultimately, the ecofeminist asks how these material walls made of loam and stone enact a deeper anxiety surrounding our very skin, our most immediate layer of self-protection; we thus confront the permeability of our bodies, feminized in their penetrability, but hardly mere objects of penetration. Through the help of small creatures and fire in this chapter, we illustrate what Stacy Alaimo has called our 'transcorporeality': how human efforts to exclude the 'outside' are futile as we are one with it, how 'the human is always intermeshed with the more-than-human world'.[5]

'Noysome and pestilent things'

Such emphasis on boundaries in and around the household (including the bodies that inhabit it) depend upon the delineations between wild/domesticated – those that align with nature/culture and female/male – of interest to ecofeminist enquiry. Or, as Jeanne Addison Roberts puts it, the association of 'Wild' with 'Forces outside that ethnic human male Cultural core':

The Wild seems to be envisioned by Shakespeare as inhabited by strange and untamed creatures, fascinating and frightening, offering the lure of the hunt with the goal of capturing or killing the Wild's imagined denizens, but at the same time as providing a reservoir of necessary resources for the maintenance of Culture. Slaves, wives, and beasts of burden are to be drawn from the Wild.[6]

While Roberts's work on the 'Wild' resonates with our ecofeminist project here, her alignment of 'wives' and nonhuman creatures remains untroubled, ultimately essentialized in her analysis rather than just in their historical association. In addition, her psychoanalytic approach means that these animals do not have a material reality outside masculinist imaginings, and as a result the animals themselves, as Puck's version of them, remain unreal.[7] More recently, a field seen to fall under the umbrella of ecocriticism, Early Modern Animal Studies, while looking at the material conditions of animals in the period, with few exceptions, does not consider the gendering that feminist theorists had previously articulated.[8] That these analyses tend to focus *either* on ecocritical *or* feminist readings leads to a certain slant as they focus on larger beings – the lions, bears, horses and deer of early modern London's environs or of the male psyche.[9] These large animals indeed populate Shakespearean drama, as *Midsummer* contains the lion through comedy, and tigers infect the tragic Rome of *Titus* even while the hunt figures significantly in both plays. Bear-baiting functions on psychological and material levels as Shakespeare's plays raise the shadow of its violence at the same time the bears actually compete for its audience.[10] Thus ecocriticism locates the material basis of the psychoanalyst's articulated anxiety and fear, emotions repeatedly regarded by Simon Estok in his theorizing of the 'ecophobia' within the plays.[11] Bears, deer and lions did not regularly inhabit most early modern London plots, however. What is more, from a theoretical standpoint, fear, including 'ecophobia', is a binary-generating feeling. While Shakespeare's tragedies depend on fear's presence and his comedies on the dispelling thereof, the focus within readings of Shakespeare on larger animals means diversion from the everyday, from the realm that is known and accommodated without fear, a realm central to ecofeminist enquiry.

As those which are encountered on a regular basis, often within one's own home, littler animals such as spiders, moths, bees, wasps, mice, cats, crickets and rats can signify interior spaces at the same time as they point to the world outside those walls. Importantly, within animal studies of late, there has been a turn towards what early modern Thomas Moffat calls the 'lesser living creatures' by critics such as Todd Borlik, Keith Botelho, Joseph Campana and Karen Raber.[12] It is our intention here, however, to illustrate the ecofeminist underpinnings of such a turn when considering Shakespeare's plays, as the difference between large animals and small ones has important gendered implications. That is, in order to consider these 'lesser living creatures' fully, critics would do well to turn to recipe books and household manuals, texts often associated with female readers and practitioners. If the home is a construct that is built upon the exclusion of the wild from within its walls, as well as its containment by way of deliberate domestication, small beings can expose the fissures in the construct of domesticity much more readily than the more overtly threatening large animals may, and in opening the way to more intimate spaces, including physical bodies, they may reorient our theoretical and methodological frame.

So rather than hunt for the panther and the hart in Shakespeare's pages, we ask what would happen if we suddenly paid close attention to the fly that interrupts the Andronici's meal?[13] How does our perception change if we ask about the rat that Hamlet attacks behind the arras or the one that Poor Tom eats or enquire about the nature of Hamlet's mousetrap? Shakespeare names two of his characters Moth (in *Midsummer* and *Love's Labour's Lost*), though only one of them is found in the wild. Yet a third is singed by Portia's candle. In turning to the small, we develop a different understanding of the human (and gendered) relationship to the environment, one that bears signs of antagonism but is at the same time intimate and enmeshed with that environment. In this turn, we can better understand and provide means of challenging and mitigating the larger antagonism and fear. The presence of smaller creatures within the domestic spaces represented on the stage denotes literal chinks in the walls of exclusion as their movement across thresholds by way of holes often thwarts attempts to regulate their entry or exit. While feminist readings may understand these openings figuratively as female desire in the hymen-regulating patriarchy, our ecofeminist readings consider this gendering materially as it goes hand-in-hand with the use and penetrability of material walls. Hamlet's rat, Portia's moth and Titus's fly as well as many other rodents and insects enter through some aperture, and their presence denotes the domestic interior at the same time it disrupts the presentation of it. The regular reminders that we are not separate from the other creatures of our environment show us how we are infused and informed by them. In the literal presence of smaller creatures, ones that are subject to human-originated pest control, we discover a perpetual co-existence rather than a tenable separation. We thus uncover how it is the delusion of their separability that motivates extermination, at the same time we witness an intimacy with the nonhuman facilitated by their persistent presence.

We see through household manuals and recipe books the first layer of walls, that which may or may not surround the garden, as these texts provide much advice towards the protection of crops. Gervase Markham's chapter from *The Second Book of The English Husbandman* entitled 'How to preserue all manner of Seeds, Hearbs, Flowers, and Fruits, from all manner of noysome and pestilent things, which deuoure and hurt them' includes, along with 'Thunder and Lightening', a long list of small creatures – caterpillars, toads, frogs, field mice, flies, green flies, gnats, pismires (ants), moles, snails, moths, cankers and garden worms – for all of which the wall is no serious obstacle. Indeed, to his husbandmen audience, Markham writes of these as if they are an encircled battalion poised to defend garden territory and attack planted seeds if necessary,

> It is not enough to bequeath and giue your séedes vnto the ground, and then immediatly to expect (without any further industrie) the fruit of your labours, no goodnesse seldome commeth with such ease: you must therefore know that when you lay your séedes in the ground, they are like so many good men amongst a world of wicked ones, and as it were inuironed and begirt with manie Armies of enemies, from which if your care and diligence doe not defend them the most, if not all, will doubtlesse perish.[14]

His use of 'inuironed' and 'begirt' connote not an actual wall, the wood or stone garden perimeter, but instead a vision of protection in which these tiny foes have the garden surrounded and only the defences of 'care and diligence' will prevail. But unlike the work of Object Oriented Ontology (OOO), which removes objects (such as walls) from their contexts, we see Markham's garden not as a series of 'ontologically prior' objects but rather as an evocation at once of the material *and* gendered qualities of their relationality.[15] With this in mind, we might think differently about the way Markham continues the military metaphor within some of the individual descriptions, describing garden snails as 'much offensive to Gardens' and *feminizing* the plants as he does so, speaking of how snails 'feed of the tender leaves of the plants' and 'of the outmost rinds of the daintiest herbs and flowers'.[16] The description of 'destroying' an anthill with 'hot scalding water' is certainly reminiscent of enemies succumbing to boiling liquids at the ramparts. Other creatures are deemed 'filthy', 'greedy', 'pernicious', and 'poisonous', 'hurting' and 'confusing' the seeds.

In defence of the garden, the male gardener is to use the dung or ash of natural predators such as falcons, plant herbal poisons such as henbane, smoke out flying things with suet fire, or sow diverting plants such as garlic and onion. We see in these defences, moreover, how the permeability of these spaces leads to positive outcomes. In protecting the plants, the garden becomes one with its defences, as the dirt absorbs the dung and its nutrients and the plants of aversion, often equally effective in strengthening the human immune system, mingle with the vulnerable seeds. The perceived threat of these creatures changes, even ameliorates, the kitchen garden. Notably, these modifications rarely mean the wholesale destruction of the insects and rodents in question; at the same time they may ameliorate the environment of which they come to be a part.

From this garden space thus feminized and transformed in its besieged state, it is an easy transition into the house itself. Indeed Markham makes the analogy between inside and outside at the end of the chapter on garden pests as he tells the gardener,

> let your owne iudgement order your Garden, like your house, and your hearbs like your furniture, placing the best in the best places, & such as are most conspicuous, and the rest according to their dignities in more inferiour roomes, remembring that your galleries, great chambers, and lodgings of state doe deserue Artes, your Hall Wainscote, and your meanest offices some ... cleanly painting: from this alligorie if you can draw any wit, you may finde without my further instruction how to frame Gardens of all sorts to your owne contentment.[17]

It is of particular importance that Markham makes this parallel at the end of his chapter because through the analogy he attempts to extend the domestication that exists within the house, the 'inferiour roomes' of its interior and associated with the housewife and her work or arts, to its exterior to be brought under the capable hands of the man of the house. His own chapter reveals the irony, however, as the pest control he deems is to be applied outside is similarly employed inside. In particular, moths, 'very pernicious in the Garden', with the same smoke used outdoors, may be driven from 'Arras hanging, Tapistrie, Néedle-worke, Cushions, or Carpets, or any woollen cloath or garment' (46). Once 'driven' from these woollen environments, however, they may then move in (re)turn to the garden, which underscores the permeability of these spaces, making moths perhaps more menacing in their virtual invisibility.

The language Markham uses in *The English Huswife* sounds disturbingly similar, but in that text it is the housewife who figures as enclosed being, seemingly bounded from within and without:

> It is meete that our English Hous-wife be a woman of great modesty and temperance as well inwardly as outwardly; inwardly, as in her behaviour and cariage towards her husband, wherein she shall shunne all violence of rage, passion, and humour, coveting lesse to direct then to bee directed, appearing euer vnto him pleasant, amiable and delightfull; and though occasion, mishaps, or the misgouernment of his will may induce her to contrarie thoughts, yet virtuously to suppresse them, and with a milde sufferance rather to call him home from his error, then with the strength of anger to abate the least sparke of his euill, calling in her minde that euill and vncomely language is deformed though vttered euen to seruants, but most monstrous and vgly when it appears before the presence of a husband: outwardly, as in her apparel and dyet, both of which she shall proportion according to the competency of her husbands estate & calling, making her circle raither straight then large, for it is a rule if we extend to the vttermost we take away increase, if we goe a hayre breadth beyond we enter into consumption: but if we preserue any part, we build strong forts against the aduersaries of fortune, prouided that such preseruation be honest and conscionable.[18]

Whereas the husband's garden is 'framed' to suit his 'contentment', the housewife is 'directed' to follow her husband's governance, making herself both 'inwardly' and 'outwardly' a reflection of temperance – a containment of will, 'passion' and 'humour' that bounds her body and her mind. Wendy Wall describes this 'superimpos[ition]' of the 'bounded domain' of the house onto the housewife as an ideal balance of 'preservation and expenditure', which draws on the general economic language of the domestic.[19] However, we want to focus here on a different sort of material connection between the housewife and material space – that of the garden earlier in Markham's book. For the martial language of domestication that we see in the passage to the husband resonates here as well, with the housewife represented as the garden in need of protection such that she figures as one among his other 'strong forts against the aduersaries of fortune'. And we see a housewife whose imperative for temperance materializes as a circle that must not be breached (from within or from without) – a 'circle raither straight than large' – lest it result in a deterioration of her very body, a 'consumption' that comes from exceeding by just a 'hayre['s] breadth' the limits established for her. At the same time, as with the garden Markham imagines, the would-be containable female, whose passions and body are to remain within established limits, threatens perpetually not so dutifully to 'suppresse' her 'contrarie' thoughts and in so doing exceeds, and thus exposes the permeability of, the very boundaries intended to secure her domestication.

Similar anxieties about the transgression of boundaries permeate recipes for pest control found in manuscript collections. With moths, as seen in Markham, it is clear that they were found in clothing. One 'To Keep Away moths Madam Tyrwhitt's', from a seventeenth-century book, seems derivative of Markham's entry in *The Second Book of The English Husbandman* and reads simply 'burne in the roome, or Chest, the hoofes of Cowes, or Calues, and lay walnut leaues between the cloths'.[20] Another, much later, shows that the 'battle' continues through the nineteenth century. In 'To destroy Moths, or to drive them from Cloth', one is to lay 'vegetable Musk Seed', prized by perfumers, 'between the folds of cloth'; the text goes on to describe how to 'destroy the Vitality of the Eggs which produce the Moths'.[21] That rats could be found among the foodstuffs is clear when reading recipes 'To Kill Rats' closely. A late seventeenth-century recipe mixes equal parts sugar, oat flour, and 'vnslaked lime' as a way of disguising the poison with the temptation; another mixes white arsenic into wheat flour and the seductive sugar.[22] The implication here is that grains and sugar were most susceptible. All of these recipes reveal the insinuation of small creatures into private spaces, within closets, pantries and chests. They are not out in the open, but within the very creases of existence. Thus the variation of the verbs in these titles – 'to keep away' vs 'destroy' or 'kill' – signifies motive as well as action. The difference between exclusion and extermination for the sake of protection of goods is not a matter of semantics; it has material consequences. For Markham's housewife as well, as she is instructed to limit her domain to the house's interior, while her husband navigates its exterior, aligning her physical body with the physical environment of the house is both potentially vulnerable to insinuation if breached from without, to excess (and 'consumption', as we see in the passage above) if breached from within.[23] But as with the small creatures that indeed penetrate the creases of the house, so too does the excessive language found in Markham's passage to his housewife betray the limits of her containment; the housewife, after all, must ultimately choose to comply (or not) with such mandates for temperate behaviour, and her compliance, like that of the rat, is by no means certain.

Each section in what follows focuses on a particular creature or thing related to domestication that manifests anxieties about control over the boundaries from within and without that seemingly govern the house: pest control (cat and mouse, followed by fleas, flies, worms, and others) and fire. Often aligned with the female body or feminized space, attempts at domestication related to the household, its creatures, and its environs reveal how the binary domestic/wild – even the 'domestic' as a category – exposes chinks in the walls.

Pest control: The scratching cat and 'the smallest monstrous mouse'

Shakespearean drama presents the material realities of the small animals among us. His plays thus expose the limits of domestic control. In particular and paradoxically, the invocation of the pest-control dyad, the cat and the mouse, reveal the entangled relations of human/nonhuman through both the pest to be controlled and unpredictable pest controller.

Mice are referenced in eleven of Shakespeare's plays, and often when they appear in the language they are shown to be in domestic spaces, making holes in walls and clothes, eating cheese, running from cats or landing in traps. Imagining himself at court, Lear cries out 'Look, look, a mouse: peace, peace, this piece of toasted cheese will do't'; and surrounded by the grand 'Nature's above art in that respect' and the throwing down of gauntlets, the smallness of the mouse signifies as an interruption of aesthetic debates and tragic action (*KL* 4.6.86–90). Figuratively, we may read the randomness of madness as a mouse crossing the room during a high ceremony; our ego-centred intentions do not dictate to all in our surroundings, and Lear's attempt to tame or trap the mouse through the cheese may be an effort to rein in both madness and his environment. Lear's outburst may be reflective of other mouse sightings, laughable tremors, as Snug beseeches the ladies 'whose gentle hearts do fear / The smallest monstrous mouse that creeps on floor' (*MND*, 5.1.216–17). These 'womanly' fears as delivered by a lion are but smaller versions of the larger ones expressed while in the woods: the snake that strangles Hermia in her sleep along with the 'monstrous' shapes Puck uses to scare the Mechanicals, and the larger fears are then pre-empted by the approach of day and the entrance of the hunt. Hippolyta's participation in the hunt thus signifies her gendered disruption, especially in light of Hermia's extreme fear of a dreamt snake; astride a horse and surrounded by hounds, she is not among the 'gentle hearts' afraid of mice. Significantly, Snug's comedic embodiment of the lion also encircles the larger fear, while Puck's blessing allays the smaller one saying that 'not a mouse / shall disturb this hallow'd house' (5.1.381–2). The entrances of mice then signify the unblessed state, one laden with material trivialities and spiritual malaise, haunted by the terrors without the city walls. The world in which mice are 'monstrous' is one that is concerned only with the 'in here', protected by walls from 'out there'.[24] Ecocritically, the inflection is clear: our environment asserts itself on our anthropocentric machinations, and these interruptions become occasions for the human having to reassert his control, his dominance. Upon ecofeminist re-evaluation, moreover, we see that the snake dreams, the wild phantasms and the monstrous mouse simultaneously evoke not only anthropocentric delusions, but also androcentric ones. These delusions are more difficult to maintain when in the wild, as Lear, Hermia and the Mechanicals discover, for in the house the mouse also 'disturbs' this invulnerable sense of self.

David Goldstein points us in this direction in his ecofeminist reading of Hannah Woolley's recipe 'For Kibed Heels', which uses the skin of a flayed mouse as a remedy. His analysis follows Sylvia Bowerbank's, hinged between two 'readings' of two mice – one, Robert Boyle's that objectifies the creature in the name of science, the other, Mary Rich's that conceptualizes it in utilitarian, if also anthropocentric terms – and provides a third possibility. Goldstein posits that Hannah Woolley's recipe, in its intimate relation with the mouse and its direct 'use value', implies a more immediate and lived relation to the environment. He writes, 'In Woolley's cosmology ... [n]ature is both "out there" and "in here" – "in here" both in the sense of inside the human and inside the house, where mice hold unwelcome court in the pantry.'[25] We consider how, in working on Woolley's rhetoric of recycling – the mouse that is caught in a trap is put to use – Goldstein's approach may skirt the larger issue, as in the same volume as the recipe 'for kibed heels' is one 'To Kill Rats', which suggests smoke will cause rats to 'forsake the Room' but not actually die (thus lying along the spectrum between 'keep away' and 'destroy').[26] Indeed, though, in all three examples discussed by Goldstein, the mouse is caught and subsequently dies, ultimately fulfilling the same material practice of eliminating the rodent that invades the pantry. In the Shakespearean examples above, Lear's toasted cheese helps us to see that pest control becomes an attempt to reassert invulnerability, to allay the disruption caused by the presence of the mouse.

The discourse of pest control in and of itself, however, may be seen to expose the delusion of containment as well, as the pest controller also becomes an agent of disruption. In returning to the *Pericles* quote above, 'The cat, with eyne of burning coal, / Now crouches 'fore the mouse's hole,' cats are mentioned in their domestic role of mouse control, as they are several times in Shakespeare's oeuvre. Cats outpace even mice in their frequency, being called upon in seventeen different plays, and all but a few references are to the domesticated kind. The quote from *Pericles* also shows the parallelism of cats with fire as both are being invited within the domestic scene, and our discussion here looks to bridge between the small creatures we have examined thus far and the housefires we examine at the end of this chapter: fires burn and cats turn. Never truly predictable, the cat moves in and out of the house, bringing with it from the outside the shadow of violence, seen in *Macbeth*'s Graymalkin, its woodland cousin. When Mercutio calls Tybalt 'Good King of Cats' and 'rat-catcher' he points to this latent violence of both man and feline and recalls this threat as he dies: 'Zounds, a dog, a rat, a mouse, a cat, to scratch a man to death.' (*RJ* 3.1.102). That this shadow is then taken as an affront by humans is the irony of domestic fantasy. Needed for their predatory and territorial instincts in pest control, cats' instincts are then denigrated if turned upon the house's human occupants – that is, if they scratch.

The 2012 Royal Shakespeare Company (RSC) production of *The Taming of the Shrew* starring Samantha Shapiro and Simon Paisley Day helps us to see clearly the gendered implications of this figuration as Petruchio 'woos' Katharina. Having taken on the challenge of marrying Katharina, Petruchio is asked by Gremio whether he would 'woo this wild-cat' (1.2.194), and interestingly, while Gremio uses the modifier 'wild', the word 'cat' alone does not necessarily represent the domestic version, as Oberon lists the 'ounce, cat, or bear' as creatures equally likely to come upon Titania in her love-drugged state. Later in the act, Petruchio thus distinguishes between the kinds of cats, as he tells Katharina he will transform her from 'a wild Kate to a Kate / Conformable as other household Kates' (2.1.270–1).[27] The pun here is that he will tame her, as from a wildcat to a domesticated one (though a wildcat is not the same as a feral one, according to the *OED*). In the Globe production, as Day delivers these lines, he hovers over Shapiro, while she is virtually pinned against the floor. In response, the woman cups her hands into claws and makes a move to scratch him.[28] While this reading may be hidden in the line, this staging reflects a deep complex of images within and around the play – cats, rape, scratching and domination – that at once expose exploitative binaries at the same time they confound them.

First, Kate's position as cat is particularly revealing given the gendered history of the word. Is the naming of a cat gender-neutral, after all? Falstaff says that he is as 'melancholy as a gib cat' (*1H4*, 1.2.73), but there is no reference to the companion doe-cat in Shakespeare's oeuvre. The *OED* provides a general figurative meaning, a 'term of contempt for a human being, especially one who scratches as a cat', citing two Shakespearean plays, *All's Well That Ends Well* and *Coriolanus*, as seventeenth-century examples.[29] The *OED*'s meaning seems unfixed, however, as it combines this umbrella term with a more specific use, 'a spiteful or backbiting woman' ('cat,' n1, 2a), and while neither of the *OED* Shakespearean examples refer specifically to a female character, the feminization of the referent (Paroles and the rabble) has interesting implications as both Bertram's and Coriolanus' positions as hyper-masculinized war heroes mark their enemies as their opposites. The connection between the literal scratching and the moral modifier 'spiteful' means that the figurative here exists on two levels, as cat comes to signify a kind of human, specifically gendered female, and the scratching becomes a metaphor for spite. In this figurative development, the cat must be at first domesticated in order for the 'backbiting' to be understood.[30] How in the next linguistic manifestation a cat is figuratively a prostitute ('cat,' n1, 2b) is a difficult leap to follow, except in that the 'cat' would be inferred as female, as prostitute in the period would be as well. This meaning, moreover, does resonate with Katharina's position as she earlier accuses her father of making her 'a stale' in the marriage marketplace (*TS* 1.1.58).

The ecofeminist significance here is that within the very conception of a cat – so typical in its scratching to come to imply it inherently – Petruchio's claims to make her as a cat/Kate 'as conformable as other household' cats/Kates reveal the breakdown in his oppositions. Literally, Petruchio intends to bring her from the wild to conformability, but the inherent nature of cats defies the distinction. The figurative negative development of the word progresses from the literal presence of cat's scratching, and we want to posit here that this negative valence within the definition of the word undoes the taming that Petruchio means to assert. To read the scratch in 'cat', as the RSC production does, is to resist its domestication.

Beyond this etymological evolution of the word are the cultural conventions of which the wife-cat analogy is a part: the depiction of the shrewish, 'unruly', or 'scolding' wife. In these conventions, the meaning of the scratch lies in the spectrum between dominance and desperation. Within the seventeenth-century print record of ballad traditions, there are many laments about or tamings of such figures, and within five there are references to women scratching as a means of asserting dominance.[31] One, 'Have Among You Good Women' (1633–69 ?), makes an overt connection to feline behaviour, 'His face She will scratch like a Cat, / and sweares what she gets she will spend', describing how some women who are reprimanded by their husbands for pawning 'his shirt and his breeches' respond. That *Taming* and such ballads are clearly connected can be seen not only in the reference to 'The Cruell Shrow' in one title (1601–1640 ?), but also in the way that both play and ballads hinge on the 'speciall care' persons must take in 'choosing a Mate', lest they are scratched and bitten like the husbands in the songs. A variation on this theme and another overt reference to scratching as an animalistic gesture – particularly catlike as the references to 'claws' in Shakespeare tend to be those of lions – is the man who chose a scolding wife, and whose 'old sweetheart' comes to visit and 'claw'd her about', causing her to go blind and to amend her ways ('The Scoulding Wife'). It is our contention that the explicit reference to cats in one ballad makes the scratching in others a kind of nonhuman behaviour, particularly feline-like, thus infusing the pun on Kate/cat with the latent violence found throughout the tradition. A sixth ballad, however, complicates the binary of scratching women as dominant and relates to the hint of coercion seen in the RSC production, because in 'The Coy Damousel Conquered; or, the Couragious Gallants Uictory' (1685–8) the damsel scratches as her only means of trying to prevent, unsuccessfully, a rape. The fact that, rather than scratch and bite as the scolding wives, she did 'scratch, squeak, and cry', which makes her scratching as inconsequential as the mouse against its tormentor and begs the question about the gendering of the cat in the first place. This cultural repetition of an alignment between women and cats as both subject to domestication and resistant to domination marks a fissure in the concomitant binaries, and the scratch is the physical, material mark of this breakdown.

Indeed, a scratch, regardless of its maker, signifies what Stacy Alaimo has called the transcorporeality of being:

> Imagining human corporeality as trans-corporeality, in which the human is always intermeshed with the more-than-human world, underlines the extent to which the substance of the human is ultimately inseparable from 'the environment.' It makes it difficult to pose nature as mere background, as Val Plumwood would put it, for the exploits of the human since 'nature' is always as close as one's own skin – perhaps even closer.[32]

In the skin acting as the last barrier to the outside world – the final wall if you will – its easy penetrability (broken by a 'dog, a rat, a mouse, or a cat') signifies the tenuous line between inside and outside that we struggle so resolutely to maintain. Mercutio's 'Ay, ay, a scratch, a scratch. Marry, 'tis enough' (*RJ* 3.1.94) and his subsequent sending for a surgeon does not downplay his own injury but rather points to a collective vulnerability, witnessed in the early modern period by the numerous recipes for skin salves meant to decrease the spread of infection in 'soares that be hott'.[33] In *Taming*, we see the association of scratching with both the breaking of boundaries and with the wild when the picture of 'Daphne roaming through a thorny wood, / Scratching her legs that one shall swear she bleeds' (Induction 2.61–2) is presented to Christopher Sly. In this offhand bit of erotica, the image of ideal static female beauty is disrupted on two fronts: Daphne's assertion of her will and the underbrush's breaking of her white skin. Again, the presence of rape in these taming scenarios underscores the real bodies subject to domination at the same time it records the resistance.

The fact that mice creep and cats (and Kates) scratch here punctuates anxieties about the vulnerabilities of the domestic spaces and the uncontrollability of female will. Through the example of mice and cats, we have seen how the domestic enclosure is both constructed and compromised through the representation of smaller creatures in the plays and the surrounding literatures, and the binaries that they seemingly represent are inherently unstable ones. In the gendering of these creatures, however, we see that the figure of the control, the cat, is unpredictable, and the human who comes to symbolize the home, the woman, is similarly an agent of her own desires. Pest control, therefore, is not simply protection against home invasion; it is an assertion of androcentric control found to be shaky even at its foundations and in the agents of its maintenance.

(Beyond) pest control: Fleas, flies and other creeping creatures

While pest control scenarios, such as the cat and mouse, highlight the material vulnerabilities of the household presented by the creeping in of creatures from the outside, one more recipe captures the profound unease with the proximity of creatures in private, personal spaces. In Anne Brumwich's mid-seventeenth-century collection can be found the following recipe written in secretary hand: 'A Medicine to kill any Quick thinge as flye or flea that is crept into *th*e eare.'[34] While the outer walls may protect the garden from large animals, winged, burrowing and smaller creatures are undaunted by such barriers. Therefore, given the opportunities presented by chimneys, broken windows, open doors and rotting wood, these creatures too make their way into the houses' interiors. Brumwich's recipe, however, reveals the real anxiety around domestic pest control: that our own bodies are vulnerable, i.e. also filled with holes.

Through the Brumwich example we can further reflect upon Alaimo's ideas of transcorporeality.[35] The recipes quoted above introduce the discomfiture of proximity, also revealed in the screeches of Snug's ladies and Markham's aggressive adjectives. What is more, it is significant that we might find the most overt articulation of this unease within a collection of medical remedies. Alaimo, too, following the work of Linda Nash, most clearly articulates her theories through a cultural analysis of Multiple Chemical Sensitivity.[36] In both early modern and contemporary examples, it is the permeability of our own bodies that most disarms us. Theories of transcorporeality help us to interrogate categories such as the domestic in our analysis, disrupting assumptions about the boundaries maintained in deference to its fantasy.

The moments in which Shakespeare's plays represent these 'lesser' creatures are bound with early modern constructions of enclosed spaces and prescribed agents at the same time as they disrupt those constructions. In revealing the mouseholes, the scratches and the canker worms, the plays show the fissures inherent in the domestic ideal otherwise seen in the tragic potentials, either latent or manifest, of the dramas. That is, the domestic is a fantasy of comedic closure, most poignantly articulated by Puck in *Midsummer* as he excludes the mice from within the house; thus the chinked wall in Pyramus and Thisbe exposes the precariousness of the division between domestic bliss and monstrous intrusion.

This is only part of the dramatic fiction, however, as the presence of tiny creatures also introduces our shared state with them. Not surprisingly, it is often the fools, in the licence they are given to speak against hierarchies, that expose us to this truth. In *King Lear*, the Fool tells the retired sovereign, 'We'll set thee to school to an ant, to teach thee / there's no labouring i'the winter.' (2.2.260–1), meaning that sometimes it is best to go underground given the constraints of time, invoking the shared state of mad kings, winter labourers and other creatures more directly subject to the elements. Most immediately, Hamlet's mad banter after his murder of Polonius underlines our shared vulnerability and transcorporeality:

Not where he eats, but where a is eaten. A certain convocation of politic worms are e'en at him. Your worm is your

only emperor for diet: we fat all creatures else to fat us, and
we fat ourselves for maggots.

(4.3.19–23)

Hamlet later echoes, 'A man may fish with the worm that hath
eat of a king, and eat / of the fish that hath fed of that worm'
(4.3.27–8).[37]

The plays thus may help us to see anxieties in material
practice, as reading Markham again through the lens of
Hamlet we understand the intensity of Markham's experiment
in worm extermination:

> Lastly, are your Garden Wormes which liuing in the
> hollowes of the earth féede much vpon your tender
> Garden séedes, and the soft sprouts which first issue
> from them, especially from all sorts of kirnels, in which
> they delight more then in any other séede whatsoe'er, as
> you may finde by experience, if you please to obserue
> accidents as they happen, without which obseruation
> you shall hardly attaine to the perfection of an excellent
> Gardner: for if you please to make this triall, take the
> kirnels of a faire sound Pippin, and deuide them into
> two parts, then lower the one halfe in a Garden bed well
> drest and trimmed for the purpose, where the worme
> hath liberty to come and goe at his pleasure, sowe the
> other halfe in some riuen boule, earthen pot, or halfe
> Tub, made for the purpose with the same earth or mould
> that the bed is, and then set the vessell so as no worme
> may come there-vnto, and you shall finde that all those
> Séedes will sprout and come forth, when hardly any one
> of those in the bed of earth will or can prosper, there
> being no other reason but the extreame gréedinesse of
> the deuouring worme, which to preuent, you shall take
> Oxe dung, and burne it to ashes, then mixe them with
> the earth where-with you couer your Séedes, and it will
> both kill the wormes, and make the Séedes sprout both
> sooner and safer.[38]

Beyond the irony that current practice recognizes the necessary presence in a healthy soil of earthworms (in the juxtaposition of the two passages from *Hamlet*, conflated with maggots), Markham's enthusiasm here surpasses that found with relation to other pests (though the boiling water on the ants is admittedly aggressive). In the propagation of the seed, the scientific controls of the enclosed container, the classification of the hollow-dwelling and extremely greedy worms, Markham seeks to conquer more than occasional pests here. In overcoming the literal garden worm, he conquers the metaphoric 'deuouring worm', i.e. death itself. Indeed, worms of all kinds confound the boundaries between inside and outside, inhabiting the body as the many recipes 'To Kill Worms' from the period testify; one from the late seventeenth-century Boyle family collection even uses an apple as bait as well.[39] It is as if both the medicine and Markham's garden are attempting to return to an imagined source: a pre-lapsarian moment that precludes death and predates a penetrable body, not only figured in the 'worm' that only eats the dead body, but also ushered in by that first worm, the serpent (*OED*, 'serpent', n. 1). Through this re-reading we can better understand the many valences of our own material practices, which are not simply, unequivocally, about preserving human life against an untimely death of starvation. The impulse to increase yield (propagating our seeds) and overcome pestilence is the race against (inevitable) mortality, an endeavour that always positions the source of that impermanence outside our bodies and that the playwright confronts most regularly.

This understanding may be extended to other modern cultural practices, moreover. Of late, agribusiness having seemingly defeated household and garden pests with toxic chemicals and pest-resistant seeds, the fear of invasion has focused on even the littler, the microscopic. In the early twenty-first century, an increased use of anti-bacterial soaps and cleansers in the household and a market-created germ obsession may have done 'more harm than good', strengthening the bacterial gene pool rather than eradicating it.[40]

Moreover, recent studies about good bacteria, the salubrious microbiome of the human digestive system, have called into question the wisdom of our cultural overdependence on antibiotics since their discovery.[41] As a result of these practices, we have depleted the nutrients of the soil, tainted the water supply and contributed to our general ill-health. And the detrimental effects of such practices are unevenly distributed across racial, classed and gendered boundaries.[42]

'The domestic' does not have to be binary-creating in the ways that we have thus far described, however. The word also may mean to be 'intimate or familiar with' (domestic 1b), and in this meaning lies artistic, as well as activist, potential. That is, Shakespeare's plays depend on this intimacy and familiarity; otherwise, the references above are felt less potently. Snug's lines about the 'monstrous mouse' are less funny for those who have been sitting socially in a rodent-free parlour. Titus's extreme reaction to the killing of a fly is made more poignant in the fact that those in his audience had certainly also swatted at the little airborne creature. The processes of pest control in the early modern period brought the householders in proximity with that which they attempted to eliminate. Our own attempts to mitigate our contact with the lesser creatures, while arguably increasingly 'effective', mean that as we attempt to hold the pests at arm's length, we also deny their place, and ours, in the biodiverse, ecological whole. As a result, we kill bees, birds and butterflies along with the tomato worms and good bacteria along with the bad. These obliterating practices depend on concerted demarcations between human and nonhuman that deny our shared transience and in the end have become increasingly harmful to the larger environment. The subsequent conversation, however, has required a reorientation of many to the microbial environment, one that theorists such as Alaimo and others have worked to integrate into our environmental-humanist understanding. What this conversation also reveals is that the domestic may hold the potential for a kind of local activism that engages intersections between environmental destruction and race, gender and class that ecofeminists have long sought to quantify and redress. In the domestic environment, the larger implications are felt deeply, wholly experienced as we make things grow, nurture our human and nonhuman constituents, cook slow food and live with cobwebs.

Between small and great, soft and fierce: The hearth

In the end, ecofeminism requires our reorientation to cultural enclosures as it asks us to pay attention to the effects of their constructions. Another example that shows the literal vulnerability of those enclosures further illuminates this process as we once again put Shakespeare's plays in dialogue with household texts. Here, we return to Puck's lines quoted above, as he attempts to strike fear in the hearts of the Mechanicals with phantasms of 'a hog, a headless bear, sometime a fire'. It is the last of these that forms the final section of our analysis as we turn from the entry of small creatures into domestic spaces to the phenomenon of house fires started in the heart, the hearth, of those spaces.[43]

Fire, of course, was a necessity of the early modern household. In the weathering of harsh winters and the cooking of meals, the household fire gave daily comfort and function to early moderns, particularly to women, who even then dominated the kitchen.[44] Fire, however, when escaping the control of the householder, was also a source of fear, as seen in Puck's lines and in the many recorded house fires of the time. Indeed, when we think of fires, we think of them in scale, from a small flame to a fireplace to bonfire to wildfire. Before turning to these incidents in which fire breaks its bounds, we will look at the ways in which household fires were a cause of vigilance and concern as articulated in early modern recipes.

Certain kinds of recipes required a close eye on the size of the fire, as a fire that burned too hot would ruin hours of work or waste a cache of expensive ingredients. In particular, the emphasis in preserve recipes on a 'small', 'gentle' or 'soft' fire reflects the delicacy of working with sugar and the need to mitigate the direct heat through several means. 'To Candy all sorts of flowers, fruits, and spices, the cleare rocke Candy' found in the anonymous print text *A Closet for Ladies and Gentlewomen* (1608) not only calls for 'a small fire of coals' under the mixture of flowers, fruits, spices and two pounds of melted Barbary sugar; it also says to take the pipkin holding this mixture and put it in a still, adding mediation between the pot and the fire. After twelve days, this leads to a flavoured rock candy.[45]

Other kinds of recipes requiring vigilance in front of the fire are various ointments, again, as the ingredients are many and sometimes expensive, but also as the burning of them may hamper the efficacy of the salve. In the affordable octavo volume *A Rich Storehouse, or Treasury for the Diseased* (1596), the recipe 'An Excellent good and approued Oyntment, for all maner of Aches, Agues, Bruses, Goutes, Cankers, Lamenes, Stitches, or hardenes of the Spleene, and for all maner of paine in the Heade and Eares' reveals its high value in the number of afflictions it may alleviate. While the herbs (sage, rue, wormwood and bay leaves) and fatty ingredients (olive oil and sheep suet) used in it are quite homely (important given the nature of the source), the amount of time and attention associated with its preparation demands a concomitant watchfulness when heat is applied:

> choppe the hearbes very smalle, and then stampe them as small as may be, then shredde the suet very fine, and put them alltogether, and then stampe the hearbes and the suet, vntill such time, as the suet cannot be perceiued, then take it foorth, and put it, into a faire panne, and put the Oyle therein, and couer it close, and soe let it stand for the space of twelue daies: then take it foorth and breake it with your handes into a brasse panne, and *set it vpon a soft fire, and you must be alwaies stirring of it*, vntill such time as the hearbes be cracklinge, then take it of and straine it

thorough a canues [canvas] cloth, into an earthen pot, and so keepe it.[46]

Here, the heat of the fire is moderated by the constant stirring, an activity recorded in many recipes to keep the ingredients from burning or, in other recipes, to keep the pot from boiling over. Thus when at the end of *Love's Labour's Lost* the winter song has 'greasy Joan' 'keel[ing] the pot' (5.2.911, 920), it is referencing a tedious recipe in which the kitchen maid must sit by the fire (thus sweaty even in the cold winter months), stirring and adding cooler water in an effort to keep the mixture from getting too hot. This attentiveness also means that the fire is kept at an even, soft level, dampened when flaring or stoked when getting too low. The precision required in many recipes for ointments, preserves, and baked goods thus determines that the size of the fire is a matter of concern.

It is of special significance, then, that the Great Fire of London was seen to begin as the result of baking bread. In another kind of domestic document, Samuel Pepys records in his diary entry of 24 February 1667 (five months after the fire itself) the report of Sir R. Vinor:

> he tells me that the Baker, son and his daughter did all swear again and again that their Oven was drawn by 10 a-clock at night. That having occasion to light a candle about 12, there was not so much fire in the bakehouse as to light a match for a candle, so as they were fain to go into another place to light it. That about 2 in the morning they felt themselves almost choked with smoke; and rising, did find the fire coming upstairs – so they rose to save themselfs; but that at that time the bavins were not on fire in the yard. So that they are, as they swear, in absolute ignorance how this fire should come – which is a strange thing, that so horrid an effect should have so mean and uncertain a beginning.[47]

While the use of 'drawn' in 'their Oven was drawn' is rare, the sense is clear that by 10 p.m., after the workday was done, the fire was depleted. When coupled with the homeliness of the evidence that candles could not be lit by the oven even as early as midnight, the testimony about the state of the fire shows a necessary vigilance as part of the baking profession, yet the fire defies its watchers. The contemporary journal entry by John Evelyn, of 3 September 1666, almost prophesies the fire's origins as he describes the 'calamitous spectacle' as follows: 'All the sky was of a fiery aspect, like the top of a burning oven, and the light seen above 40 miles round about for many nights.'[48] While the Great Fire is the fire that comes to mind most with relation to the early moderns, house fires were common, given the chimney and architectural technologies of the time as well as the early modern dependency on hearthwork in their daily diet and heat regulation. Most notably, Pepys recorded fifteen fires in his diary as well as providing one of the most detailed accounts of the Fire.[49] On the other side, Pepys also often records a 'good fire' as if giving testimony to his own domestic and economic well-being. Indeed, he reflects upon the scarcity of domestic comfort through the lack of such a fire, having found his wife dining at his father's house as 'we not having one coal of fire in the house, and it being very hard frosty weather'.[50]

The image of domesticity, the 'fire in the house' – the wife by the hearth, the daughter baking bread, the kitchen maid stirring the ointment – is the opposite of the horrors of the Great Fire that destroyed so many homes, but these reports show how one is contained within, may even be the source, of the other. We can see this throughout the figurative language of the period, as, for example, Anna Trapnel decries against 'university learning' that 'looseth its great bands' in *The Cry of a Stone* (1654, notably before the Great Fire), drawing on material experience: 'For in the Chimny the fire is / useful and precious, / But when the rafters it doth reach, / it sets on fire the house.'[51] Evelyn and Pepys both document how the Great Fire caused the ultimate disruption of the household, with furniture and persons being displaced into the Thames, fleeing at the last possible minute in order to save as much of their household goods as they could. These images of fire, as that which at once represents domestic spaces at the same time as it evokes the threat of their dismantling, is a regular occurrence within Shakespeare's plays.

It is not surprising, then, that various characters throughout the oeuvre invoke fire as an image of the well-maintained domesticity as well as of hospitality and well-being. Frequently, the characters who summon the image are low figures – clowns, servants and fools – thus least likely to take a warm hearth for granted. Lavatch, in *All's Well That Ends Well*, whose name connotes low-born in both the French word for cow (*la vache*) and the English weed vetch (Frenchified for the setting), speaks for this homeliness when he comes upon Paroles: 'I am a woodland fellow, sir, that always loved a great fire, and the master I speak of ever keeps a good fire;' (4.5.46–48). Petruchio in *The Taming of the Shrew* gives his servant Grumio the task of riding ahead and starting a fire, upon which Grumio comments:

> I am sent before to make a fire, and they are coming after to warm them. Now, were not I a little pot and soon hot, my very lips might freeze to my teeth, my tongue to the roof of my mouth, my heart in my belly, ere I should come by a fire to thaw me. But I with blowing the fire shall warm myself, for, considering the weather, a taller man than I will take cold.
>
> (4.1.3–10)

In *King Henry IV, Part Two*, Mistress Quickly, the comedic keeper of the hearth, reminds Falstaff of the domestic comfort she has given him, though for a fee, at the same time as she threatens to take it away by having him arrested:

> Thou didst swear to me upon a parcelgilt goblet, sitting in my Dolphin chamber, at the round table, by a sea-coal fire, upon Wednesday in Wheeson week, when the Prince broke thy head for liking his father to singing-man of Windsor

– thou didst swear me then, as I was washing thy wound, to marry me, and make me my lady thy wife.
(2.1.86–92)

And in *The Merry Wives of Windsor*, she promises to reward 'honest, willing, kind' John Rugby for his help with a scheme with 'a posset ... soon at night, in faith, at the latter end of a sea-coal fire' (1.4.7–8), the implication being that the 'sea-coal fire' in both instances parallels the 'comfort' of Mistress Quickly's sex. Lear's Fool doesn't let the image stand without a negative valence, however, as he asserts, 'Truth's a dog that must to kennel; he must be whipped out, when the Lady Brach may stand by the fire and stink' (*KL* 1.4.109–11). Importantly, many of these characters speak to their social superiors as a way of reminding them that 'a good fire' should not be taken for granted, as Paroles, Falstaff and Lear variously discover. Indeed, the withdrawal of creature comforts adds weight to the boy's joke about the dying Falstaff that Bardolph should 'put [his] face between his sheets and do the office of a warming-pan' (*H5* 2.1.83–4).

Through the invocation of a warm hearth in the middle of tragedy, often the ghost of domestic bliss may be raised in bald juxtaposition to the current cold moment. After his deposition, Richard disrupts the future comforts of his loved ones by telling the Queen:

> In winter's tedious nights sit by the fire
> With good old folks, and let them tell thee tales
> Of woeful ages long ago betid;
> And ere thou bid good night, to quite their griefs,
> Tell thou the lamentable tale of me
> And send the hearers weeping to their beds;
>
> (*R2* 5.1.40–5)

Martius raises the image of those who remain blissfully ignorant of the fires of war yet deign to challenge political decisions through images of domesticity:

> They'll sit by th' fire, and presume to know
> What's done i' th' Capitol: who's like to rise,
> Who thrives, and who declines; side factions, and give out
> Conjectural marriages
>
> (*Cor* 1.1.190–3)

While not in a tragedy, in the dire outlook of the battle of Agincourt, the 'watchful fires' of Henry V's men are reminiscent of the tavern fires left behind in the *King Henry IV* plays (*H5* 4.0.23). In *Lear*, the lack of fire and hospitality comes to represent the onset of the tragedy. The fool, no longer at Goneril's house, out in the storm imagines 'old lecher's heart, a small spark, all the rest on's body cold' (*KL* 3.4.110–12). The 'walking fire' that then enters is Gloucester, bringing with him the image of the caregiving abandoned by the elder daughters:

> My duty cannot suffer
> T'obey in all your daughters' hard commands.
> Though their injunction be to bar my doors
> And let this tyrannous night take hold upon you,
> Yet have I ventured to come seek you out,
> And bring you where both fire and food is ready.
>
> (*KL* 3.4.144–9)

Cordelia then echoes language she never hears by seeing the atrocities of the previous act as the ultimate double disruption of the domestic ideal through the biting domesticated animal and the threatened absence of fire: 'Mine enemy's dog / Though he had bit me should have stood that night / Against my fire' (*KL* 4.7.36–8). These characters are so far removed from the comforts of warm fire, loving family and loyal dog (the fantasy called up in all of these examples) that that ideal's distance is part of the impact of the lines.

Similarly, the threat of a raging fire may be invoked in the comedies to indicate the tragic potential in some actions. In *The Two Gentlemen of Verona*, the waiting woman Lucetta responds to Julia's 'Thou wouldst as soon go kindle fire with snow / As seek to quench the fire of love with words' with 'I do not seek to quench your love's hot fire, / But qualify the fire's extreme rage, / Lest it should burn above the bounds of reason' (2.7.19–23). As a comedic woman of lower status, Lucetta tends to the fire, 'qualifies' it – keeps it within reason. Similar to Lucetta's image but differently infused is Cressida's question to Pandarus about Cassandra's laughter in the scene over Troilus's chin hairs: 'But there was more temperate fire under the pot of her eyes. Did her eyes run o'er too?' (*TC* 1.2.143–4). In this quip, Cressida puns on Pandarus' description of Hecuba's eyes that 'r[a]n o'er' with laughing; she also reflects the domestic knowledge held in the recipe books that a small or soft fire keeps the mixture from boiling too fast. Essentially, her words look to cool Pandarus' ardour, an ardour she herself shares but dares not voice. The whole of the play, moreover, shows the effects of an untempered passion, a pot that has boiled over, quenching the fire and spoiling the stew. Lucetta's and Cressida's vigilance in front of the live fire of youthful passion is as women's labour sitting and regulating the strength of fires in making medicines and preserves. Moreover, as with the oven that started the Great Fire, it is the abandoned fire that sparks an entire city. Thus the Puck figure at the end of *Merry Wives* looks to pinch those maids where fires are found 'unraked' (5.5.44), i.e. where coals may be left burning. An ecofeminist reading tends to these fires as they are being managed (usually by women) and not only when they are out of control, because in the contained version lies the embers of the fire out of bounds, to which we turn next.

The histories and tragedies in particular draw on the real early modern material fear of an uncontrolled domestic fire to underline the import of the moment. They also recontextualize the fire in a way that emphasizes its perverse or harmful potential. The examples of domestic fires summoned for perverse means are the pyres to which Leontes would 'commit' both Paulina and his infant daughter in *The Winter's Tale*, the sacrifice of Alarbus in *Titus*, Calpurnia's ingesting of hot coals in *Julius Caesar* and the fire under the witches' cauldron in *Macbeth*. Wendy Wall's analysis of the last of these and the 'demonic domestic' is important here,[52] and ecofeminists would add to these domestic perversions moments in which a domestic fire is figured as getting out of control because these moments are often represented in gendered terms.

Most notably these moments occur in the middle of the fires of war, pointedly within the male sphere. For example, at the very beginning of *King Henry IV, Part Two*, upon hearing the news of his son's death, Northumberland joins the rebellion in an extended (and admittedly confusing) metaphor:

> as the wretch whose fever-weak'ned joints,
> Like strengthless hinges, buckle under life,
> Impatient of his fit, breaks like a fire
> Out of his keeper's arms, even so my limbs,
> Weaken'd with grief, being now enrag'd with grief,
> Are thrice themselves.
>
> (1.1.140–4)

The image is of a sick man (importantly hot with fever) who rages against his caregiver because of his frustration; for Northumberland, purportedly sick, the image works less as analogy and more through proximity. The fire simile here, however, is embedded in the longer metaphor, as the sick men 'break … like fire', becoming 'thrice themselves'. The embedded image is thus for the rebellion growing as a fire grows when sparking on to tinder. In *King Henry VI, Part Two*, Queen Margaret, a character who clearly defies gender norms in the histories, uses a similar image to describe rebellion in Ireland: 'Nay, then, this spark will prove a raging fire / If wind and fuel be brought to feed it with' (3.1.301–2). John of Gaunt in the later-written history describes Richard II as if he was a rebel within his own kingdom: 'His rash fierce blaze of riot cannot last. / For violent fires soon burn out themselves' (*R2* 2.1.33–4). As worn as it may seem, moreover, what remains striking about this imagery is that it draws upon the literal language of war, that is, that which simply describes what is happening. Cominius speaks of Coriolanus and his plans for 'th' fire / Of burning Rome' (*Cor* 5.1.13–14). In the nascent rebellions surrounding Henry IV, the new king reports that 'the rebels have consumed with fire / Our town of Cicester in Gloucestershire' (*R2* 5.6.2–3), and leader of the peasants' revolt, Jack Cade tells his comrades to 'go / and set London bridge on fire; and, if you can, burn / down the Tower too' (*2H6* 4.6.13–15). Fire's use as a literal weapon of war makes it an apt metaphor for the passions that fuel it, but these passions and these fires are set against the smaller fires and everyday concerns. So with many of our allusive examples here such as the 'watchful fires' of the English camps and Martius' derision of the protestors, as well as most references in the histories, fire is a locus that draws tension between the binary of war and domesticity. This analysis demonstrates that it is not 'nature' or the nonhuman that opposes the domestic, but rather the pointedly human realm of war.

Domestic enclosures are that which war purportedly seeks to protect – just think of Henry V's threats at the walls of Harfleur – at the same time it ultimately disrupts that construction for those in the middle of it. In working with Wall's considerations of both household and nationalistic categories, we might say that Henry V brings war to France in order to keep it out of England.[53] Thus war may be read as the anti-domestic at the same time as it is in part fuelled (so to speak) by the maintenance of certain domestic ideals. All of these examples, however, construct fire wholly as a tool within the human realm rather than that which defies human control and supervision.

As noted above, many early modern wildfires were not intentionally started, resulting in a sense of fear and powerlessness with relation to the constructs of domesticity that are not focused on that which lies outside but rather that which exists within one's four walls. We see this most clearly in Pepys description of the Great Fire, but even fifty years before, Iago, when telling Roderigo to raise the alarum around Othello's and Desdemona's marriage, uses the following simile: 'Do, with like timorous accent and dire yell / As when by night and negligence the fire / Is spied in populous cities' (*Oth* 1.1.74–6). The details here reveal the voice of experience, one that has heard such cries and been warned against said 'negligence'. Iago's 'by night and negligence' brings out the real fear, that while we sleep, we may find ourselves 'choked with smoke'. Such 'smoke' and 'fire', though, in *Othello* and elsewhere in Shakespeare, also evokes the sinuous female body out of control. Here, the fire that ranges in 'populous cities' is Desdemona herself, having eloped with Othello. And the notion of an overheated female body, ranging wild, recalls anxieties prevalent in the period about the dangers of women's passions remaining unchecked, about their balanced humoral state depending on their being moist and cold, not too 'hot' (as Leontes accuses the innocent Hermione) and thus uncontained and not 'natural'.

After the fire

Recently, these fires are recognizably our own doing, as severe droughts have made city limits susceptible and protests have been accelerated by deep-rooted frustration, destroying businesses, multimillion dollar homes, and human and nonhuman lives. The desire to point fingers, direct/deflect blame, in such instances as Markham at the ramparts, reflect a desire to keep the threat outside, the pestilence without. This unruly threat, moreover, may be gendered female, as we see in the case of the Hayman fire of Colorado, 2002. A *Denver Post* article, written ten years after the fire, begins:

> If you know the story of the Hayman fire – which ... grew so large it dropped ash like plump snowflakes on downtown Denver – you probably know this: Forest

> Service worker Terry Lynn Barton admitted to accidentally starting the blaze when, in a moment of emotional distress, she lit a letter from her estranged husband in a remote campfire ring near Lake George.[54]

The article goes on to raise certain suspicions circulated in the court hearings following the fire that Barton in fact intentionally started the fire. Regardless, she 'lit the match' during a season of a fire ban, a day that 'was windy – gusts to 35 mph near Lake George – and hot. The humidity was eight percent. Grasses, shrubs and trees were brittle dry.' Like the baker in 1666, she testified that she 'watched [the lit letter] till it burned out completely' and that she 'thought it was out'. A plea agreement meant that the forest caretaker would serve five 'lonely years' in prison, conflicting statements left unresolved.

Whether or not the story of the fire's origins is true, it provides an interesting postscript to the early modern relation to fire. A woman, passions out of bounds (a Julia without a Lucetta), lights a match that sets thousands of acres aflame. The subsequent heroism of the four men and one woman who died battling the blaze would be juxtaposed with the 'lonely', love-distressed service worker who started it. Hidden in this narrative, however, is the place of the environment: the grasses, shrubs and trees poised to be set ablaze by a lightning strike or a careless camper as so many have been set before and since. Obscured by the female antagonist is the natural cycle of forests, once-lush green made brittle by beetles and lack of rain, ready to be ignited, a cycle made more dramatic by the severity of the droughts resulting from climate change.

The focus on human tragedy and villainy reasserts the binaries underlying an us-versus-them narrative. The dream home is pitted against the fire that seeks to consume it. If we reconsider the situation through the lens of the shepherd Corin – 'the property of rain is to wet, and fire to burn' (*AYL*, 3.2.25) – we do not downgrade the work of those who risk life and limb to protect home, hearth and human life, nor do we absolve all arson and negligence that begin specific blazes. We do, however, start to see our cohabitation with the elements. Building in evergreen forests, as those in the American West have done increasingly, we must negotiate that terrain with extreme vigilance, cutting away dead shrubs, filling bathtubs and evacuating immediately. Fire is a literal reminder of the poststructural edict that 'the walls of domestic enclosure that would separate human from nature and define human as such are nowhere to be found, as human corporeality and textuality effortlessly extend into the more-than-human world'.[55] The fire does not have us in mind, but we must be mindful of our intimacy with it in order to live where we do.

On the other side of the Hayman fire, we find the burn area beautifully flourishing. Charred trunks of pines jutting from flower-filled meadows, an invitation to bird species such as the Lewis's Woodpecker – pink-breasted and emerald-winged – that have not been seen in the area since the many years of forestry work that preceded the fire. From its peaks, one sees no edifices, only the tangled dirt routes that negotiate the climb to this new beauty.

Returning to Shakespeare's plays, the persistence of household pests and the threat of house fires signal a human vulnerability that the fantasy of the household seeks to keep at bay. The practices of seasonal and diurnal vigilance – spreading ash on the soil, planting garlic or rue, laying musk seed in the woollens, keeling the pot and raking the coals – do not seek to undo this vulnerability so much as they acknowledge it on a regular basis. Cultural exercises that seek to obliterate the enemy invader or find someone to blame also look to deny our shared and finite place in our environment and that 'the "human" is always already part of an active, often unpredictable, material world'.[56]

3

How we know any thing

CORDELIA *Nothing, my lord.*

LEAR *Nothing?*

CORDELIA *Nothing.*[1]

The deceptions of the senses must be referred to the particular inquiries concerning sense and the objects of sense, excepting only that grand deception of the senses, in that they draw the lines of nature with reference to man and not with reference to the universe; and this is not to be corrected except by reason and universal philosophy.[2]

A weakened sense of the reality of our embeddedness in nature is seen in the cultural phenomenon of ecological denial which refuses to admit the reality and seriousness of the ecological crisis.[3]

This chapter explores three plays in which Shakespeare 'destabilize[s] worlds of thinking with other worlds of thinking', as Donna Haraway articulates it, and challenges ways of knowing that rely on and support such categories as 'supernatural' and 'natural'. These plays show how both women and nonhumans possess agency inherent in a knowledge characterized not by the distinct subject/object relationship, where each stands as separate from another, but rather by a mutually constitutive 'endosymbiotic' intraconnectedness whose articulation lies beyond what might be known.[4] By looking at *King Lear*, *All's Well That Ends Well* and *Macbeth*, this chapter argues that Shakespeare's works can insist on a holistic approach to the relationship between human and nonhuman, that the result of revaluing embeddedness rather than objectivity (or separation) is that both women and the nonhuman are imbued with agency that defies human (and male) control. These plays, that is, show how 'knowing' cannot be reducible to a cerebral or even sensual (in Baconian terms) relationship, defined and articulable, between knower and known. 'Knowing' is akin to an experiential intraconnection between and among 'things', where what is 'known' is not quantified but ineffable, ephemeral.

Nothing is everything

An ecofeminist approach to Shakespeare's *King Lear* proves an ideal starting place to understand in fresh ways how the play (and Shakespeare more broadly) engages with shifting discourses about knowledge and the relationship between human and nonhuman 'things'. Rather than a sense of bounded identity, the play reorients forms of knowledge to emphasize an embeddedness of the human/nonhuman suggestive of what Stacy Alaimo calls 'transcorporeality' (as we have discussed more at length elsewhere in this book), or how the human is corporeally 'intermeshed with the more-than-human world', even co-produced by and with rather than subject of/over it.[5]

In this way, an ecofeminist reading here diverges considerably from ecocritical scholarship on the play, which tends to emphasize instead the 'strained relationship between human bodies and the non-human environment', not their fundamental interconnectedness.[6] Such a reading is possible if we take the ageing King Lear as our primary focus, which is understandable to a large degree and tempting to be sure. He is, of course, the title character of the play, its tragic hero. Even ecocritics, whose declared aim is to decentre the human, might consider the importance of, say, the storm as a meteorological event rather than just a manifestation of Lear's internal turmoil, but they spend numerous pages explicating almost exclusively the complexities of *his* (largely self-induced) tragedy. As some have recently pointed out, though, Lear's singular importance is actually *de-emphasized* in the play – as indication of resistance to human exceptionalism, as Laurie Shannon writes,[7] or to lament human 'alienation from the biophysical world', as Todd Borlik argues.[8] But by focusing in particular on Lear, even to show how the play uses his character to challenge the notion of human exceptionalism or anthropocentrism, scholars risk reifying the 'human' as a universal (and dominant, and male) category. That is, even as ecocritical scholars seem to deconstruct a model of human exceptionalism by showing how the play resists it, making Lear the primary focus of analysis under-represents (even ignores) *how* the play enacts such resistance. Such ecocritical work may seek to trouble the human/nonhuman binary, but unless we also elucidate how such a binary is linked to gender and class, as the play also does, we ultimately reinforce the disenfranchisement of women, the poor, and the nonhuman for which the play serves as a corrective.

King Lear helps us trouble this binary, as it resists the subject–object relationship inherent to dominant modes of knowledge (and that allows for defined categories of natural and supernatural) and moves instead towards the murkier territory of wonder, the fuzzy terrain of embedded experience.[9] The play turns away from the privileging of the 'thing' to be known, and the centrality of the privatized, commodified 'thing', as we are reminded early in the play and at the end that it is instead 'nothing', or 'no thing' that is quantifiable, an epistemology of which might be traceable. Rather, it is the ontological co-evolution of 'things' as co-agents that is not only cellular, but also cultural and includes labour relations, class positions and gendered identities.[10] While the play begins with a focus on Lear and land that might be privatized and distributed, it exchanges the primacy of the individual for the prominence of the organism in the sense that human and nonhuman are characterized not as discrete categories but as intraconnected elements of the same, collectively comprised whole that revalues the importance of women, the poor and the nonhuman as integral, agentic participants.

More than just depicting Lear as vulnerable to the elements, the storm scene in particular demonstrates his transition from resistance to recognition of this vulnerability. Lear first curses the storm, attempting to command it as he has (unsuccessfully) attempted to command heavens, the earth and the beings that inhabit it throughout the play. He famously cries out,

> Blow winds and crack your cheeks! Rage, blow!
> You cataracts and hurricanoes, spout
> Till you have drenched our steeples, drowned the cocks!
> You sulphurous and thought-executing fires,
> Vaunt-couriers of oak-cleaving thunderbolts,
> Singe my white head! And thou, all-shaking thunder,
> Strike flat the thick rotundity o' the world,
> Crack nature's moulds, all germens spill at once
> That make ingrateful man!
>
> (3.2.1–9)

Here, Lear attempts to assert control over the storm, demanding that it act upon him, that it 'blow', 'rage', 'singe', 'strike', 'crack' and otherwise employ its full force against his ageing and weary body. By commanding as Lear does, he tries to position himself as sovereign over the elements much as he does when the play opens and he executes what he calls his 'darker purpose' and pledges to divide the kingdom into three parts (1.1.35–9). In a decision that catalyses much of the tragic action in the play, Lear makes a critical miscalculation, one that he repeats early in the storm: he believes that he has control over the nonhuman – first, land, and, later, the elements themselves. In the case of the former, power to distribute (and reconstitute boundaries of) the land he occupies; in the case of the latter, power to command a meteorological phenomenon that transpires having nothing to do with his words.

The storm prompts an awareness that Lear's power is at its core a delusion. Having refused (for a second time) to enter the hovel that might shelter him from the storm's intensity, Lear speaks quite differently than before, though:

> [*Kneels*] Poor naked wretches, wheresoe'er you are,
> That bide the pelting of this pitiless storm,
> How shall your houseless heads and unfed sides,
> Your looped and windowed raggedness, defend you
> From seasons such as these? O, I have ta'en
> Too little care of this. Take physic, pomp,
> Expose thyself to feel what wretches feel,
> That thou mayst shake the superflux to them
> And show the heavens more just.
>
> (3.4.28–36)

What Lear expresses here, catalysed by the rain's smarting torrent on his skin, is that he has not (or at least has not as fully or in the same way) until now engaged with empathy or compassion; experiencing the 'pelting' of the 'seasons', the points of contact where the elements and his skin meet, reorients him to his inherent vulnerability rather than his presumed dominance and creates the conditions for a different perspective. In other words, our inclination to focus on Lear as a human subject perhaps betrays our own proclivity toward human exceptionalism. The pelting elements act as co-agents in the scene, forcing Lear to move away from a focus on self and instead towards (human and nonhuman) Other. As the play shows, and as scholars have commented on, Lear's 'too little care' is characterized by a human arrogance over the things of nature. But what scholars have discussed much less often is how such arrogance is simultaneously towards the poor and women such that the human exceptionalism rejected by the play applies equally (and at the same moment) to hierarchies of human over human *and* human over nonhuman.[11] They are, as this moment demonstrates, part and parcel of the same deluded notion of power. We might recall, that is, that Lear's attempts to allot land are directly connected to his desire to control his daughters, to dictate their affections. And just as Lear identifies with the 'poor naked wretches' that experience the same rain, the same seasons as he does (in the sense of seasonal variation as well as the human 'seasons', or lifespan, that remind Lear of his mortality), the pelting rain that slaps and soaks his skin underscores not humans' 'separation from the nonhuman world', as Steve Mentz has maintained,[12] but rather their interconnection. Lear removes his clothing, which in effect, undoes this separation; he encounters the elements unmediated to where its moisture becomes his skin's, enacting the transcorporeality at the heart of Stacy Alaimo's recent theorization.[13] Lear and the rain are enmeshed in a transcorporeal relationship by which the boundaries between one and the other blur; and, as the play demonstrates, Lear's recognition of such transcorporeality occurs at the same time as he recognizes the same of his relationship with his fellow humans, the 'Poor naked wretches' who are like, *who are*, he – subject to the same pelting rain, the same cycle of mortality. And we might also note that when he does so, according to the stage directions he also kneels, falling prostrate at the foot of those over whom he has considered himself to that point sovereign – the earth, the elements, the poor. What *Lear* stages, then, is akin to what we might call 'environmental justice' today, that which is also of import to ecofeminist politics and scholarship.

But if we stop with Lear, or even if he remains our primary focus (*his* failings, *his* discoveries), then we miss the point. After all, other characters in the play 'get' what Lear comes too late to understand, only they are marginalized or ignored. In particular, Cordelia and Edgar-as-Poor Tom articulate and value a connection between themselves and the nonhuman world, a linkage that environmental justice (and ecofeminism) contends troubles binaries related to humans and nonhumans (and women and the poor) that allow for the human subjection of human and nonhuman Others. And both value answers to pressing questions derived from everyday experience, from that embeddedness of human–nonhuman interconnection rather than their separation by way of natural philosophical explanation or a belief in the supernatural. When Lear asks Poor Tom, for instance, 'What is the cause of thunder?' and enquires about his 'study', Poor Tom replies, 'How to prevent the fiend and to kill vermin', locating his knowledge source in a mad kind of household work, even though he is technically homeless; this is not the work of the gods or the scientists (3.4.151, 154–5). And when Lear calls Poor Tom his 'philosopher', Tom responds with a most practical, visceral, 'Tom's a-cold' (3.4.167–8), underscoring his clear interconnection with the elements. We might also recall that when donning the disguise of Poor Tom, Edgar adopts what he describes as the 'basest and most poorest shape' of man while hiding in the hollow of a tree (2.2.181), as if adopting the outer casing of his natural environment as his own outer bodily layer. He takes as his example the 'Bedlam beggars, who, with roaring voices, / Strike in their numbed and mortified bare arms / Pins, wooden pricks, nails, sprigs of rosemary' (2.2.188–90). In their voicing, these poor men and women enact the permeability of their skin. It is as if in their madness and in Poor Tom's homelessness, they have become especially open to their transcorporeal relationship with their surroundings.

Cordelia is differently associated with embedded knowledge – in her case, the medicinal cures that a housewife might concoct to heal the sick in her household connote an intimacy with the natural world that is not performed but rather enacted. Cordelia describes Lear in his altered state, crowned with wild plants, which she identifies as 'rank fumiter and furrow-weeds,

/ With burdocks, hemlock, nettles, cuckoo-flowers, / Darnel and all the idle weeds that grow / In our sustaining corn' (4.4.3–6).[14] The plants she describes, all of which would likely grow plentifully in the English countryside, have medicinal uses that range from diuretics and purgatives to ingredients for ointments or even poisons. Her identifying the plants followed by her instructions to the others in the scene to 'Be aidant and remediate / In the good man's distress' (4.4.17–18) suggest that her concern for Lear's welfare goes beyond his psychological state and are pointed as much to his physical health. Cordelia begins her directive to 'remediate' Lear with the claim that 'All blest secrets, / All you unpublished virtues of the earth, / Spring with my tears' (4.4.15–17). That is, Cordelia links the 'unpublished virtues' of the earth itself with her own corporeality, her 'tears'.[15] The cure for Lear's madness is embodied jointly in herself and the nonhuman world.

This remedy evokes the many such cures found in recipe books in the period, where practitioner and plant (or animal or mineral) were necessarily part of interconnected ecological and cultural systems. A recipe from the book of Mistress Corlyon, a woman of whose life we know little other than the extensive collections associated with her cookery and medicine, is evidence of such embodiment:

A Medecine for a Pinn and a Webb or any other soore Eye

Take one handfull of three leaued grasse, that is most spotted with white: Gather it cloose to the roote, as much of wilde dasye rootes ^and after^ Stampe them all in a wooden dishe, and boyle them in one pinte of water, in a clean brasse skillett with a very softe fier. When it is scommed, put in so much Allome as will make the water tast roughe vppon your tounge. After putt in so much honny as will make it looke yeollow, and tast very sweete. When it hath boyled a pretty while and is cleane scommed, straine it into any cleane vessell, and when it is colde power the clearest into a glass, and keepe it in a colde place, and it will last three weekes in Winter, and 14 dayes in the Sommer: The water is to be applied to the Eyes one hower before they rise, and when they goe to bedd. If the Eye be very soore, dress it at two of the clocke in the after noone, and sleepe after it, if they cann.[16]

As this recipe demonstrates, to create a remedy is to enact intimate connections between human and nonhuman material. The woman who might make this recipe 'gather[s]' the white-spotted grass 'close to the roote', for instance. The patient (or practitioner) applies the ointment to the ailing eyes. This intimacy also expresses multiple forms of agency. It is hardly as simple or straightforward as merely reading and applying directions; the female practitioner must discern one grass from another (here, the one with the white spots) as she gathers and judges how close to the root to sever the plant; she decides when the water she uses is yellow enough and 'taste[s] very sweete'. But the materials and nonhuman environment she engages possess agency as well: the richness of the honey, for example, is the result of a mingling of substances both plant and bee, and the shelf life of the ointment the recipe details depends not only on the woman's effectiveness in making it, but also on temperature variations that go hand-in-hand with seasonal change. The body of the patient, too, exhibits agency, as the relative pain in the eyes dictates the amount of the application, and the patient's ability to sleep affects the recipe's efficacy.

Such an intimate (though not romanticized) relationship between and with humans and nonhumans experienced as part of women's domestic medicine was at the heart of what early modern science aimed to deny. Early modern scientific discourse, predicated on the distance between subject and object, between knower and known, is confounded by the embedded experiential relationship between them. In place of what she identifies as a masculinist mode of objectivity associated with modern (and early modern) science – the 'transcendence and splitting of subject and object' – Donna

Haraway argues for a 'feminist objectivity' that involves revaluing of 'situated knowledges' and 'partial perspectives', those derived from embodied (and embedded) experience.[17] 'Situated knowledges', Haraway posits, 'require that the object of knowledge be pictured as an actor or agent, not as a screen or a ground or a resource, never finally as slave to the master that closes off the dialectic in his unique agency and authorship of "objective" knowledge'.[18] By taking seriously the knowledge embodied in women's recipes and understanding them as expressions not only of women's work practices that we might revalue but also of 'situated knowledges' that underscore agency of multiple kinds (human and nonhuman), we might in turn reorient ourselves to broader frameworks related to agency that we find in the period, especially subject/object and natural/supernatural.

As we see with Cordelia's response to Lear's ailment, Shakespeare's *Lear* pushes us in the direction of such 'situated knowledges' over the increasingly dominant notions of objectivity associated with early modern science. Cordelia's remediation of Lear's seeming madness also works to deconstruct the natural/supernatural binary, offering yet another example of a third, alternative, category.[19] Thinking about this play from an ecofeminist perspective, then, might also change the way we understand the relationship between humans and the 'natural' and thus Lear's madness. What if madness is expressed in the play as an alternative way of being, a state of transcorporeality derived from an and/both interconnection between human and nonhuman? That is, while mad, Lear is out of sorts, unable any more to differentiate in ways he had before: his hierarchical authority as father or king, his privileged standing as human over the nonhuman world. But if indeed the play moves towards this alternative mode of being, one that values transcorporeal connection between humans and nonhumans, then isn't it also a move *towards* madness? If so, then madness is not a state to be lamented or feared, but rather a release from what the play may be suggesting is a primary human (and dominant masculinist) delusion: that such categories can be bounded or cordoned off in the first place, the mouseless room of the previous chapter. What if, in other words, being mad does not cause Lear to lose everything or even just express loss, but rather it is the precondition for his recognition of that which he never had?

We might recall that Lear's 'madness' emerges most fully during the storm scene, where scholars have often discussed the storm in terms of Lear's emotional unrest.[20] Even ecocritics have suggested that the storm scene punctuates Lear's separation from the nonhuman world.[21] But if the moments when the play seems most clearly to identify Lear as mad occur at the same time as he experiences (and acknowledges) his transcorporeal connection with the rain, with the nonhuman, and with the poor, then would not his state of madness in fact also be a heightened state not of disconnect but of belonging – not, as he believes early in the play, to a world based on the notion of hierarchy (whether political, familial, gendered, classed and/or human over nonhuman), but rather to an integrated, organic whole where human and nonhuman (and categories of class and gender) dissolve into one another, their boundaries indistinguishable? The relationship Lear evokes is not one of distanced subject/object but rather intimately interlocking subject–object where the boundary between them is indistinct.

Lear speaks in such terms while aiming to comfort Cordelia when they are taken as prisoners. She laments, 'We are not the first / Who with best meaning have incurred the worst' (5.3.3–4), to which he responds by telling her,

> We two alone will sing like birds i'the cage.
> When thou dost ask me blessing I'll kneel down
> And ask of thee forgiveness. So we'll live
> And pray, and sing, and tell old tales, and laugh
> At gilded butterflies, and hear poor rogues
> Talk of court news.
>
> (5.3.9–14)

In this scene, Lear subjects himself to Cordelia, kneeling (as he does earlier when he becomes subject to the pelting storm) and positioning himself at the level not of father or king but as fellow (and fallen) human; but Lear and Cordelia are simultaneously connected with the nonhuman world, both 'birds i'the cage' and, a few lines later, 'like foxes' who are hunted and smoked out of their holes (5.3.9, 23). As when he is unclothed in the rain, identifying with the poor and acknowledging his subjection to and embeddedness with the elements, Lear here is articulating an empathy with the caged and hunted. He and Cordelia are hardly dominating human subjects over dominated nonhuman objects; their knowledge of the nonhuman is not one of distance but of intraconnection, of similitude.

If we take an ecofeminist approach to *King Lear*, we can see that the tragedy of the play may not so much be the fall of a once-great monarch or the dissolution of familial bonds, but rather the destabilization of a fundamental human arrogance that leads to a simultaneous domination of the nonhuman, the poor and women alike. Bearing Cordelia, dead, in his arms, Lear says, 'She's dead as earth' (5.3.258). In this most intimate moment, Lear punctuates what the play demonstrates over and over again: we are (and not just will eventually be) earth. And, if we are to believe the stage direction, he proceeds to lay her down, on earth (even though it is stage-as-earth), as if to underscore this fact. If indeed the play does present us with such a framework, then hierarchies of various sorts come undone: class, gender and human/nonhuman in particular. The play, therefore, advocates for a sensitivity to the priorities of what we today might call environmental justice, insisting that such hierarchies are destructive to all involved. Lear may come to realize this midway through the play, but Edgar (as Poor Tom) and, perhaps especially Cordelia, seem to understand it all along. In Cordelia's response to Lear's demand in the first scene of the play to link her love for her father to land acquisition, Cordelia repeats, simply, 'Nothing':

LEAR Strive to be interested, what can you say to draw

	A third more opulent than your sisters? Speak.
CORDELIA	Nothing, my lord.
LEAR	Nothing?
CORDELIA	Nothing.
LEAR	How, nothing will come of nothing.

(1.1.85–90)

Cordelia's 'Nothing' negates the value Lear places in land-as-commodity (and daughters likewise), the notion that either humans or nonhumans can/should be acquired, dominated, hierarchized. Lear's emphasis on people and places as 'things' to be possessed and distributed becomes 'no' thing – that is, not things in Lear's sense, but, as we see later in the play, constitutive parts of a larger organic whole, invested with value in their own right, apart from human acquisition, possession and/or domination. While Lear misses the irony in his 'nothing will come of nothing' (he is indeed correct, just not in the way he means early on), he realizes only too late that in the end, the human body is nothing more than earth, and that earth and the nonhuman things that inhabit it can no more be dispersed or traded than the humans that reside on it. In *Lear*, then, to 'know' a 'thing' is to experience it, to embody with/it; and 'nothing' is indeed everything.

Unknowability

Shakespeare's *All's Well that Ends Well* similarly meditates upon the embodied and blurred relation between subject and object and further deconstructs what it means to 'know' a 'thing'. In the play, we know the following: the King is ill; his doctors have been unable to cure him; Helena comes from modest beginnings; Helena has a book of recipes she inherited from her father; the King is ultimately cured. *How* this cure happens, however, and the source of agency and authority for the cure remains unknown and, for all purposes, unknowable. Such unknowability is a great source of anxiety in the play, but it is also the primary source of power. And in this play, that power associated with the unknown is linked most directly with women and the nonhuman. As such, the play troubles developing and increasingly dominant ideas about the subject–object relationship inherent to early modern scientific discourse, whereby 'the 'object' is treated as passive, the one acted upon, and the knower is the active party who extracts knowledge from the reluctant or mute object.[22]

In *All's Well*, the agentic source of the king's cure eludes the inquisition of doctors and audience members alike; the king is cured, and, again, we *do not know* how or why. Is the king cured because Helena's father's recipe made it happen? Perhaps. Is he cured because of the experiential practice of Helena, whose implementation of the recipe is the source of the healing power? Maybe. Is his cure the result of the healing agents – the plants, animals and minerals – themselves? Who knows? We do not and cannot know. By leaving the answers inconclusive, the play pushes us not to choose one category as an answer, nor does it just beg ambiguity, but rather it compels us towards a third category in which the transcorporeality in *Lear* is realized in a different way – here it is the intersectionality, the intraconnection of human and nonhuman revolving around women and nonhuman nature through domestic labour, akin to what Haraway calls the 'tentacular', which sees the relationship not as teleological but rather as a web of interconnectedness. That is, the play suggests that the intraconnection between human and nonhuman happens not by way of that which we identify as male, but rather through the practice of Helena – or other female or male practitioners of domestic medicine – and plants, animals and minerals.

Helena's cure of the king evokes such intraconnection in the ambiguous character of its details and in the unlocatable source of power, both of which suggest its tentacular rather than teleological qualities. Mary Floyd-Wilson argues for the 'hidden' qualities of Helena's cure, but for Floyd-Wilson the power associated with the unknown, the wonder it calls to mind, is the mystery inherent to the recipe and to the practice (Helena's as well as her father's) upon which it is predicated.[23] But to argue thusly elides the agency the play affords both women and material ingredients; the efficacy and power that the play suggests may also be inherent to the human user–nonhuman relationship; or, the specific connection between Helena and materials enacted/embodied in that experience of curing may be where the mystery and wonder lies, such that women and plants, animals and minerals are mutual purveyors of this mystery, upon whom/which the wonder depends. We hear great things about Helena's father, renowned doctor Gerard de Narbon,[24] whom the Countess recounts as one whose 'skill was / almost as great as his honesty' and 'would have nature immortal'; and Lafew calls him 'excellent', echoing the Countess by insisting 'he / Was skilful enough to have liv'd still, if knowledge / could be set up against mortality' (1.1.17–18, 28–9). Gerard de Narbon's skill, it would seem, has no parallel, but he does not in fact cure the king, as we well know, because he is dead before the play even begins. Helena has only the remains of her father's practice, the textual residue of what experience and training provided him.

Such facts make all the more significant, then, Helena's famous speech that concludes the same scene:

> Our remedies oft in ourselves do lie,
> Which we ascribe to heaven; the fated sky
> Gives us free scope; only doth backward pull
> Our slow designs when we ourselves are dull ...
> The mightiest space in fortune nature brings
> To join like likes, and kiss like native things.
> Impossible be strange attempts to those
> That weigh their pains in sense, and do suppose
> What hath been cannot be. Who ever strove
> To show her merit that did miss her love?
> The king's disease – my project may deceive me,
> But my intents are fix'd, and will not leave me.
> (1.1.216–19, 222–29)

It seems rather conspicuous that Helena, who had been present but silent during the praise of her father's practice, finishes the scene alone and claims the efficacy of 'remedies' from quite a different source. For Helena, 'remedies' lie not in the extant texts that seemingly just articulate them; rather, they are embodied in the individuals curing and cured, in the way 'nature brings' together 'likes' to effect a cure, and the wonder of what of the process/products/cured body remains beyond what is known. Those who venture not to imagine alternative possibilities, who 'do suppose / What hath been cannot be', who perceive based on 'sense' as a means to the end (the Baconian meaning), neglect to see the power of the 'strange attempt' itself. As Helena articulates here, the remedy lies somewhere betwixt and between – in the interstices of the simple calculus of the recipe, its application by the practitioner and the ingredients themselves. As such, Helena seems to suggest multiple sources of agency, including male and female humans as well as personified Nature and nonhuman ingredients. What Helena underscores here is not an isolatable source but rather the confluence of multiple sources and agents characterized not by what might be known but rather what remains a wonder. The only thing that seems clear is that the power is not attributed to a singular supernatural or natural entity.

Such reckoning of the unknown squares with how Helena describes the particular recipe for a fistula that she aims to use to cure the king. On the one hand, Helena establishes her father's book as an authoritative source, his 'prescriptions / Of rare and prov'd effects', she says, are 'such as his reading / And manifest experience had collected / For general sovereignty' (1.3.218–21), which echoes claims of Gerard de Narbon's skill by the Countess and Lafew earlier in this scene. But of the specific contents of the book, she says, they are 'As notes whose faculties inclusive were / More than they were in note' and that 'There's something in't / More than my father's skill' (1.3.223–24, 239–40). Helena's father seems indisputably to have possessed great skill, and his book many 'secrets' with 'prov'd effects', but wherein lies the power of those cures? As Helena repeats in her 'more than', the power seems a good bit more complicated than simply the 'notes' she or anyone else might apply. The notes themselves have 'faculties', it would seem, though the 'faculties' are not constrained by the materiality of the note, the textual details of the recipe. So, who/what are the agents of the cure?

Indeed, it could be argued that Helena says what she says so that, rather than being asked to hand over the recipe, she appears to be the only one who can cure the king. As Catherine Field writes, 'the king's fistula becomes a magnet for anxieties about a woman's specialized knowledge, knowledge that is suspiciously transgressive in its power to mend a frail monarch's body'.[25] But from whence does this transgressive power come, and what is the result of it in the play? According to Field, the cure validates the 'newly emerging scientific empiricism at odds with the superstitious and religious view of the natural world'.[26] However, for that to be so, we would expect to see Helena as an empiricist, the recipe itself a source of quantified and repeatable details. But as Helena's 'more than' implies, this is not the case. At least not clearly and definitively the case. Instead, we experience a gap in time between the conversation Helena has with the king and the declaration the king is cured. What happens in-between? It is this unaccounted-for space between, whose details remain uncertain, that we argue is of import to understanding how and why the king is cured. And in asking us to attend to this gap the play emphasizes not existing ways of thinking (either those 'superstitious' or 'scientific' that have as yet seemed the only viable options for reading the play) but rather alternative frameworks of knowing. In particular, these alternatives require us to take seriously possibilities for different sources of power and agency as well as a range of implications they may point to.

Such multiple possibilities, miracles, are inherent to the way recipes worked in the period. Take the recipe for a fistula in the receipt book of Lady Frances Catchmay (c. 1625):

An Excelent healinge drinke to cure, all mannor of wowndes, fistulaes, vlcers, in the bodye or owld soores.

Take of Sanicle, Bugle, Cumfrey, Ribworte, daysies rootes and all wood Bittony, Scabias, Egremony, Spedwell, Avens, Bramble toopes, of each of all thes one good handfull, but of the Cumfrey and Bugle more then of any of the rest and for want of Cumfrey in the winter take the rootes, picke and washe all thes yearbs very cleane and shred them very smale, then put them into eyght quartes of fayre running water in a cleane potte and sett them on the fier and let them boyle sowftely fowr or five howers, when it hath so well boyled put into it a quarte of white wine and so lett it boyle a little while, then put in a pound of the best english honney and let it boyle a quarter of an hower after it, then take it from the fier and let it stand in the potte all night and in the morninge streyne it and keape it for your Vse. it will in the sommer continue good a forthnight and in the winter longer, when it waxeth sower, you must have new drinke in readines, for any wound or other soore you must take five, seaven, or nine sponfulls at one time in the morning fastinge and the like quantitye att thre a clocke in the after none and so continue takinge it vntill you be well if the greafe be aboue, the fewer sponfulls at one time is best, but if it be belowe, then the most is best you must washe any greafe with the drinke that is owtward and if you see cause you must tente it for a time. This drinke hath done strange cures on fistulaes and other inward and owtward greafes, but the time must be attended with patience so little quantitye of drinke cannot do wonders on a soddayne and a greater quantitye is not so good, for it will souer passe through the bodye.[27]

This recipe contains many of the typical qualities of directions for cures in the period that evoke the sort of and/both third category that is the subject of this chapter. As with most recipes, including the Corlyon that we discussed earlier, this one draws on multiple sources: the human practitioner, whose discretion is required to discern, for instance, the quantity of a 'good handful' or how long a 'little while' would entail for boiling, and the nonhuman, the seasons, which affect how long the cure will keep, and the plants and wine, whose tendency to 'sower' after a period cause the practitioner to make a new batch. But also key to this recipe is its expression of mystery, of the 'strange cures' that it has effected in the past and promises to do so again, those that defy what the directions and ingredients seem to control. What is written on the page, only tells us so much. This cure, as we might understand all cures, depends on 'wonders' as well as what is known. The words on the page might seem to limit possibilities – we are told to use particular plants, not others, to employ certain methods of production (boiling and not distilling, for instance), to apply the remedy in defined amounts and at specified times of day – but as the 'strange cures' and 'wonders' imply, the possible explanations for how and why the cure works are multiple, perhaps limitless.

When Helena persuades the king to allow her to cure him, and in the absence of explanations about how he is cured, we witness these multiple possibilities.[28] Helena's insistence that she (and only she) can bring about the cure would seem to locate the answer in her own agency. Even before Helena effects a cure, Lafew tells the king that she has 'amaz'd' with her 'wisdom and constancy', which establishes an authority for Helena based not strictly on her father's book and enables her to employ a 'medicine / That's able to breathe life into a stone, / Quicken a rock, and make [the king] dance canary / With sprightly fire and motion,' whose 'simple touch' might resurrect a dead king (2.1.83, 2.1.71–5). Helena certainly acknowledges the cures in her father's book, which she promises to 'tender', and alternately offers 'heaven' and her father's recipes as legitimizing her claims to help the ailing king. But she suggests as quickly that it is perhaps in her 'appliance' of said cures that the king will find relief (2.1.103–57), and when he agrees to let Helena try to help him, he calls her 'Sweet practiser' and says, 'thy physic I will try', moving further away from the supernatural (heavenly) to more codified forms of knowledge by male physicians (2.1.184). It is her practice, it appears, and she as practitioner, to whom we might attribute the king's restoration to health.

But even that single explanation is resisted by the play; instead, Helena's practice is but one explanation among several (or many). Instead, Helena employs the notion of mystery to persuade the King to let her heal him, and his recovery seems attributable as much perhaps to the sort of 'strange cures' or 'wonders' explicated in the Catchmay recipe for fistulas. When offering her curative services, Helena tells the king,

> Great floods have flown
> From simple sources, and great seas have dried
> When miracles have by the great'st been denied
> Oft expectation fails, and most oft there
> Where most it promises, and oft it hits
> Where hope is coldest and despair most fits.
>
> (2.1.138–43)

In other words, even as she promises a cure, Helena proffers no clear explanation of it. The 'expectation' to which Helena refers appears to be that which explains the inexplicable – the 'miracles' that defy human apprehension. The 'Great floods' from 'simple sources' may seem to refer to Helena, but they may just as well refer to the natural phenomenon as-yet articulated or quantified – the seasons, the ingredients, etc. – especially given the punning on 'simples' as herbs that circulates throughout the play. Helena is in effect requiring the king to believe in miracles, and the play may well be pushing us to do the same.

Although Lafew sides with religion, interprets Helena's cure as a 'heavenly effect in an earthly actor', and rejects what he terms the 'modern' approach by 'philosophical persons' who make 'familiar' what is unknown, and although the king calls Helena his 'preserver,' the play is a bit more sketchy about clear attribution (2.3.1–6, 48). We know simply that the king is cured. As with the recipe in the Catchmay book, the absences that accompany the king's cure are as significant as that which appears readily available on the page. Many scholars have noted the odd nature of the king's entirely offstage cure, but most have taken the ambiguity related to it and attributed to it facts that we get only in fleeting moments earlier – that Gerard de Narbon's skill is remarked upon, that Helena and others comment that his book contains rare and effective 'receipts', or even that Helena is called a practitioner. But as with recipes from the period, there is plenty of import to the details that remain unstated, unclear. Just as recipes call for a practitioner's discretion in what constitutes sweet or what is more than a handful of comfrey and bugle, the play retains the possibility that it is not Helena's father's book, the 'notes' within it, that contains the important bits of healing but rather Helena's use of said book. That is, the 'notes' contain the schematics, but Helena must improvise so that she as practitioner is the agent, not the object.

But we also know from recipe books that the plant, animal and mineral ingredients themselves contain curative properties, and early moderns would not necessarily have balked at the notion that nonhuman things used in cures *do* something. And so, by having the action entirely offstage, the play also leaves open the possibility that the nonhuman ingredients Helena used in the cure may themselves have effected the sort of 'miracles' that Helena described earlier. What is significant is that none of these options is clearly foreclosed, all are left as potentially viable. Indeed, what is perhaps more significant still is the fact that all of these options hinge upon an embedded interrelationship between Helena and nonhuman things. That is, Helena has already explained that her father's book is not enough, that the cure entails 'more than' the notes in it, but it is the interrelationship suggested by the act of curing, of using nonhuman ingredients that necessitates Helena's being both a user-agent of medicinal plants/animals/minerals and the plants/animals/minerals themselves acting as agents in the complex chemical process that defies ready explanation – the 'miracle' of which Helena speaks earlier. It is both Helena and plants/animals/minerals, the 'and/both' that inspires wonder, characterizes the power inherent to what is at present and will likely never in the future be fully known.

'Howe'er you come to know it'

Shakespeare's *Macbeth* illustrates a similar approach to the and/both of *All's Well* as it further queries how we might 'know' a 'thing'. Like *All's Well*, the play proposes an alternative category, an and/both constituted by embeddedness within the nonhuman world that in turn deconstructs the supernatural/natural boundary and gestures towards the 'not-yet-known' rather than objective truths. The play's opening, with the witches' incantation, highlights an ambiguity associated with them and their relationship with the nonhuman world that evokes broader questions about the relationship between humans and nonhumans in general.[29] Begging more questions than they resolve, the witches discuss what seems to be at once a time and no time, a place and no place in particular, and a state of being simultaneously material and ethereal. We know not, that is, whether they will meet 'In thunder, lightning, or in rain', only that it 'will be ere the set of sun', a rather vague referent indeed. And the 'Weird Sisters' seem compelled to act by the calls of their animal familiars, Graymalkin and Paddock, the cat and the toad invoked here with all of their domestic-disturbing, scratching and poisoning potentials, leaving them to exit 'through the fog' (1.1.1–12).

Soon after this opening follows the first meeting of the Weird Sisters with Macbeth and Banquo – as promised, on the heath – whereby the witches seem uninterpretable within conventional paradigms of either gender and the categories of supernatural and natural, and the play thus articulates an alternative category of existence that may be a source of anxiety within the world of Dunsinane but also, the play suggests, may represent an authentic form of knowledge and experience not found in books. Banquo's attempts to interpret what/whom he sees on the heath confounds his relationship both to the gendered human and the nonhuman worlds simultaneously.

> What are these,
> So wither'd and so wild in their attire,
> That look not like th'inhabitants o'th'earth,
> And yet are on't? Live you? or are you aught
> That man may question? You seem to understand me,
> By each at once her choppy finger laying
> Upon her skinny lips: you should be women,
> And yet your beards forbid me to interpret
> That you are so.
>
> (1.3.39–47)

In one breath, he queries the sisters' place relative to the earth, the material soil humans would, Banquo assumes, occupy; but his questioning of their earthly status is followed immediately by, and thus linked to, his inability to pin down their sexed identity – they 'should be women', Banquo asserts, but their 'beards' defy such assignations. Rather than being 'neither/nor', these sisters exists in a realm of and/both, and therein lies their power; they may not look like other earthly inhabitants, but they inhabit the earth; and they are indeed female (the play genders them so throughout), even if their 'beards' baffle Banquo's interpreting them thusly.

More than this, Banquo's 'What are these' prompts a line of thinking that mimics the sort of monological reasoning that Val Plumwood associates with 'hegemonic forms that establish, naturalise, and reinforce privilege' that the play rejects and exchanges for a sort of dialogical, relational way of knowing that is dependent upon embeddedness and not distance.[30] For Plumwood, a 'monological form of rationality' is foundational to modern (and early modern) science and stems from a drive to 'hyper-separate ourselves from nature and reduce it conceptually in order to justify domination'. This hyperseparation, underscored by the subject/object binary, relates to an 'historical rationalist imaginary' in which 'women and other "lesser beings" are the Others of reason' and 'which is treated as the province of elite men who are above the base material sphere of daily life and are entitled to transcend it because of their greater share in Reason'.[31] Shakespeare's play makes a similar connection: Banquo's query, 'What are these?' refers at once to the sisters' gendered identity and their relationship to the earth and, by querying as he does, he attempts to apply a reasoned explanation of both. That is, he aims to know, and thus to re-demarcate, the boundaries between human and nonhuman, and between male and female that human/nonhuman implies.

But Banquo, importantly, does not get what he wants. Instead, he is unable to interpret, it seems, not because he is necessarily incapable of applying reason to the moment, but rather because the witches defy interpretation. In their confounding of categories, the witches operate as agents and 'forbid [Banquo] to interpret' their status. Banquo's questioning, while it aims to position the witches as object of his enquiry, reverses and shows the sisters instead to be subjects in their own right. The line between subject and object blurs. But it is important to note that in the play such reversal within the human gendered realm is inextricably linked to a similar reversal related to the human–nonhuman subject–object relationship. Banquo's inability to interpret their gender is tied to his inability to interpret their status as human. This frustration may heighten Banquo's anxiety, and later Macbeth's, but it also heightens their (the women's and the earth's) power; that is, to ask whether a creature is male/female or human/nonhuman is to aim not only to define (and subject) the 'Other' under scrutiny but the self as well. The witches' uncertain status thus destabilizes Banquo's (and by extension other males' and other humans' in the play) status, causing him to wonder if he and Macbeth have 'eaten on the insane root' (1.3.84) and in turn serves to deconstruct the binary within which such status is defined in the first place.

We learn shortly after that Duncan's murder was signalled not only by the prescient witches, but also by the nonhuman alarums of his death: the wolf (Duncan's 'sentinel'), owl, crickets, falcon and Duncan's horses (2.1.53, 2.2.3, 2.2.15, 2.4.1–17). Even the earth itself and the stones Macbeth treads upon will signal, Macbeth fears, his dark deed: 'Thou sure and firm-set earth, / Hear not my steps, which way they walk, for fear / Thy very stones prate of my where-about' (2.1.56–8). And, following Duncan's murder, we learn that the 'night [itself] has been unruly:' (2.3.54). Both to signal and to foretell, at least with any accuracy, are the domain of women and the nonhuman in particular in this play, not men who employ what would resonate with early modern scientific thinking.

An ecofeminist reading of the play thus compels us to reorient ourselves to the weird sisters, to the other-than-human, which brings us to a vision of the world that is about multiplicity, possibility, one that embraces wonder and the not-yet-known. Repeating their famous incantation ('double, double, toil and trouble'), the witches use nonhuman ingredients in such a way that evokes women's domestic medicine and cookery. Wendy Wall, for instance, makes the point that the ingredients indeed resemble those found in kitchen cookery and concludes that the play's evocation of domestic work 'demonizes an already alarming domestic practice' by calling attention to the wicked associations of the ingredients themselves.[32] While it may be tempting to understand their ('hell') broth as a sign of the supernatural, of demonic engagement, or 'sinister', as Wall asserts, we should remember that the animal parts – and human-parts-as-animal – in it are merely 'ingredience'; the play only applies the word 'wicked' to *Macbeth* when the sisters see him enter, only after he claims to 'conjure' them (4.1.45, 50) along with their skilled knowledge, 'howe'er [they] come to know it'.[33] The witches call their brew a 'charm', but its effects might be better understood as something more than supernatural; the source of their knowledge and power, along with the effects of their labour appear to be the machinations of the liminal figures – not quite human, not quite nonhuman – more than a spirit or divine. When Macbeth recognizes the interconnection of their practice with winds and 'Nature's germens' (4.1.59), or invisible life-giving seeds (employing, we might note, some of the same words that Lear does in his attempt to command the storm), he calls out the wondrous elephant in the room: we may be too quick to define the sisters' work as sinister – their 'ingredience' are simply creatures that walk the earth; they are not those of darkness, and these 'Natures germens tumble all together' to concoct an ontologically co-evolving collective of material and (women's) labour that defies the very 'answer' Macbeth (and the audience) would like. We know, that is, that apparitions follow, which the sisters appear to summon, but the relationship between the visions and their (human or nonhuman) agents is unclear. They are, as Macbeth's 'germens' suggests, not reducible to an answer but to the awe and vulnerability of wonder, of the not knowing. And therein lies their power.

In this reorientation around not knowing, *Macbeth* embraces a version of the preternatural that celebrates, as Loraine Daston writes, the 'strange': 'strange weather, figured stones, petrifying springs, the occult virtues of plants and minerals, and myriad other deviations from the ordinary course of nature [whereby] [m]arvels were not so much violations of as exceptions to the natural order'.[34] To stand in wonder is to accept partial understanding and a 'situated knowledge', a knowledge dependent on the embedded relationship between subject and object and that embraces multiple possible sources of agency – nonhuman and human alike. And it is this sort of knowledge that is associated with the feminized if not entirely female, mainly the weird sisters, throughout the play.

Macbeth's downfall ultimately stems from hubris that is not finally attributable to his kingly ambitions but his rejection (or at least lack of recognition) of his own embeddedness, his own rejection of this wonder. He believes in a version of the 'natural' that separates humans from nonhumans, that sees nonhumans as objects distanced and controllable, which in turn leads him to see humans likewise. And so, if we focus on Macbeth, we are reminded of this flawed vision and to some extent become similarly tragic participants in it; he and Banquo ask, for instance 'What is' while the play explodes possible options for 'what might be'.

The power of and in uncertainty

At a time when so many Humanities faculty are having to justify the 'skills' students learn in our classes, what they 'know' as a result of our syllabi, this reorientation to the not-yet-known seems all the more relevant. The vocational emphasis imposed by so many legislators in states across the US (and elsewhere) constitutes simply a different way of moving us away from wonder, towards a version of the known that appears quantifiable, reducible; it is also contrary to the very skills that are foundational to the Humanities, where we teach students the value of multiplicity, of that which eludes capture in our conception or by textual representation, of empathy, which is at its heart recognition of embeddedness with another, whether that other is human or nonhuman. In spring 2015, *The Chronicle of Higher Education* published a piece about Jonathan Gottschall, a PhD in English who struggled for years to find a tenure-line position to no avail. His story, one the writer describes as 'how brash literary Darwinists and evolutionary theorists attempted to "save" English departments – by forcing them to adopt scientific methodology – and were, on the whole, repelled', speaks to a situation all too familiar to us today.[35] Gottschall, himself a 'literary Darwinist', laments the refusal of English departments to see the necessity of incorporating (masculine) scientific methodologies into literary studies to transform what he calls 'feminized in spirit' current practices and curricula into something more legitimate. What this article evokes is how the broader tension between Humanities and STEM disciplines relates to how we value different ways of knowing. What Gottschall sees as 'feminized' is the very multiplicity of ideas and perspectives that is foundational to the Humanities as a discipline; so what scientific methodologies presumably grant the Humanities is a path towards certainty, away from the imagined towards the real.

Such devaluing of the Humanities may well undermine our purpose if we aim to find more sustainable ways of living on this planet with other humans and nonhumans. Redressing our over-consumption of resources, for instance, through technological means is not necessarily a bad thing, but it cannot be our only recourse. Developing alternative technologies to replace depleted natural resources may allow us to continue living the way we do on this planet, but at what long-term costs? Those same technologies help maintain the illusion that humans can perpetually use nonhumans (and other humans) *as* resources; they mask what the plays we discussed here expose, that such an approach is hubris. We are not proposing that the Humanities displace STEM. Far from it. But if we are to learn anything from thinking about ecofeminist theory and Shakespeare, it will at least be that addressing our current ecological crises will necessarily involve challenging ourselves to live in fundamentally different ways on this planet, which will in turn require that we revalue different ways men and women have lived on and with other humans and nonhumans in the past as well as how many still do so today. We will need to embrace multiple ways of knowing, an and/both orientation and inclusive approach to our different disciplines that might help us know more fully in ways that are also embodied and embedded. We need too to embrace and revalue what we do not yet know, what we might never know, for in the not-yet-known is power and possibility that meets the what-seems-to-be with the what-may-be. The power of and in uncertainty.

4

The dynamic object

[L]ife was but a flower[1]

*[I]n the month of may in a morning before sunrise
wipe of the dew of green wheat*[2]

[T]he stone is right[3]

The indifference of stone

Filled with remorse for the irreparable damage, the deaths, he has caused, Leontes asks a purportedly inanimate thing to speak – 'Chide me, dear stone, that I may say indeed / Thou art Hermione' (*WT* 5.3.24–5). He goes on to imbue the stone's very silence with subjectivity – 'or rather, thou art she / In thy not chiding; for she was as tender / As infancy and grace.' (5.3.25–7). Thus, in its silence, the carved stone decidedly becomes un-stonelike – 'tender' as the state of childhood or divine benevolence – as it is inhabited by an idealized feminine spirit, albeit Leontes' version of her, her subjectivity as 'Hermione' resulting from his having said so. Those in attendance proceed to detect 'motion' and 'breath' in what is apparently motionless and inert. Even as the audience recognizes the actor playing Hermione while the action unfolds, it is held between Paulina's and Leontes' vision, not knowing if s/he is a statue or living, not certain, that is, if the Hermione on stage is Paulina's, Leontes' or her own. Ironically, throughout the discussion, the actor stands, indeed breathing, as motionless as s/he can be for the minutes under performance. Leontes may seem to summon Hermione's lifeless self into an idealized version of being, but peel back the layers of the ostensible conundrum – was Hermione dead all these years to be resurrected from her memorialized form or hidden away from tyranny? – and we are reminded that what appeared lifeless had life all along.

This tension – that regardless of the debate around it, the figure on the stage lives and has an existence aside from that existence being declared as such by another – provides an interesting allegory for the ecocritical crossroads that looks to posthumanism and Object Oriented Ontology as a means of confronting an anthropocentric world view. In turning away from the human subject, ecocritics turn to the agency of objects in the 'more than human' world. These theories envision the 'vibrancy of matter', as Jane Bennett has called it, or alternately imagine, in Ian Bogost's words, an 'alien phenomenology' – 'what it's like to be a thing' – acknowledging that the closest one can get is through metaphorization and anthropomorphizing.[4] That is, like Leontes' projection onto the statue, our understanding of a given object is limited by what we already know – what our memory and experience make of it by way of cognitive connection with things – and as a result, our own subjective perception, our own remorse, comes into play. The bigger irony ultimately arises that if the stone were to talk, it wouldn't necessarily talk to us, no matter how deserving we would be of its chiding. At the very least, as Barbara Johnson so rightly asserts, 'The stone can't defend itself against anthropomorphism without resorting to anthropomorphism.'[5]

Ecofeminism, though, sees the gendering of this allegory as also key to understanding its tensions. It is no coincidence that the not-speaking-but-imagined-living stone is given a female subjectivity, one which is 'silent' in its grace and ideal because 'not chiding'. Readings of the scene from *The Winter's Tale* such as Leonard Barkan's and Barbara Roche Rico's have noted the Pygmalion-esque projection onto the living statue,[6] while others have seen an interplay with post-Reformation iconography;[7] the particular feminist implications in line with both of these understandings, however, are clear as the statue embodies the alabaster- and marble-skin of Petrarchan conventions, making Hermione into an icon of 'impossible perfection'.[8] To the feminist reading of sonnet convention, ecofeminism adds another layer and sees the scene as doubly reifying: woman becomes object at the same time that the object becomes feminized. Not only does Hermione seemingly become fixed in perfection as a silent statue (ironically nothing like her eloquent self in Act 3), but also the stone becomes woman-like (though like no woman we've seen in *The Winter's Tale*), tender and silent. The fact that aged Hermione lives (no thanks to Leontes' words and actions) undoes this Petrarchan reification.

Further consideration of the scene as an allegory for an ecocritical conundrum, moreover, shows how the objects exposed to posthumanist enquiry (here represented by Hermione's statue) are similarly feminized, inaudible because imagined and spoken for, and, as feminist theory has elucidated, illustrative of the place of women in certain artistic paradigms such as Petrarchism for centuries. Given the work done by feminist criticism of the eighties and nineties, we must ask if we can possibly divorce a discussion of 'objects as other' from a history of the 'objectification of the other'. Ecofeminism looks at moments of object-orientedness as thus disturbingly retrograde even if, in theory, apparently forward-thinking.

For this reason, we draw on the notion of 'affordances', as ecological psychologist Harry Heft understands them, but to them we add our particular emphasis on gender.[9] Experienced by way of perceptual rather than conceptual engagement with another, subject–object relations become not fixed in (human) comprehension; instead, our experience as/with things is dynamic and transactional. Heft's work reminds us that we can no more articulate a pre-cognitive (or extra-cognitive) relation between things than we can recuperate an intellectually pure 'thing'. Understood in this way, we might necessarily conclude that 'things' are always part of a complex and shifting web of meanings, materialized through both bodies and environments and bound within systems of value. Heft's notion of 'affordances' thus allows us to account for how gendered subjectivity, for instance, relates to posthumanist notions of 'thing' power.

In the early modern period, one place where we find this equation of women with nature, with 'natural' objects, is in the language of eros, and here we turn to interrogate Petrarchism, which is paradoxically both at the centre of the allegory we discussed earlier and evidence of the 'challenge of reification' articulated by Heft.[10] This chapter thus dismantles a familiar Petrarchan trope from its material origins. Here we mean not the 'object-oriented feminist ontology', or 'weird essentialism' Timothy Morton espouses,[11] but rather a materialist ecofeminism that accounts for the entangled qualities of the social and ecological (rather than biological) of the sort Heft describes – the tactile, affective, dynamic, and co-experiential encounters between humans and other things in/with environments. In our reconsideration of plants within the blazon tradition and recent theoretical discussions of the object, we also present seemingly inanimate vegetable matter as more than it seems, imbued with labour and discrimination, use and abuse, integrally part of the economies in which it circulates, but more than fixed commodities to be purchased or discarded. Thinking about plants historically as within transactional relations with humans, labour and consumption reminds us that the human–nonhuman (and male–female relationship within Petrarchan discourse) is not one of acquiring and consuming the thing, but rather the intra-active, cross-boundary interdependency that disrupts the very binaries gendered subjectivity presumes.

Dynamism in the garden

In one of the most influential pieces of feminist scholarship that examines the blazon tradition of the early eighties, 'Diana Described', Nancy J. Vickers argues that 'bodies fetishized by a poetic voice logically do not have a voice of their own'[12] and writes,

> Laura is always presented as a part or parts of a woman. When more than one part figures in a single poem, a sequential, inclusive ordering is never stressed. Her textures are those of metals and stones: her image is that of a collection of exquisitely beautiful disassociated objects.[13]

Vickers analyses how the blazon tradition at once mutilates and silences the female love object, and in it she underlines the objective of objectification: 'his speech requires her silence', which in effect is the impact of Leontes' tyranny over his wife and idealization of the silent statue.[14] Thus feminist readings of the period have considered the woman's standpoint: in *Twelfth Night*, Olivia deconstructs the commodification of her various parts, 'item, two lips, indifferent red; item, two / grey eyes, with lids to them; item, one neck, one chin, / and so forth' (1.5.241–3),[15] or more directly, in *Pamphilia to Amphilanthus*, Lady Mary Wroth writes a whole sequence inhabiting and challenging Petrarchan models. What Vickers' analysis and others like it, however, do not consider is the way in which the tradition conceptualizes and thus limits along with the beloved, the things to which the beloved is being compared. Ecofeminism would most want to trouble the categories that reduce women and nonhumans, and in order to do so we need to trouble reductive practices and recuperate the histories that demonstrate both women and the things to which they are compared to be quite animate all along. Even to say that the female beloved is given the 'textures ... of stones' as if it were a negative thing is to perform an unfairness to the stone itself that carries with it, as Jeffrey Jerome Cohen has so intimately delineated, a many-coloured and multi-surfaced millennial history and, depending on its kind, can be either porous or smooth, crumbling or hard, opaque or crystalline, matte or opalescent, etc.[16] Each stone holds a dynamic relationship to its geological and historical context and cannot be reduced to a circumscribed concept, any more than a human, male or female, may be.

Leaving stones aside for the moment, this chapter looks to another focus that carries with it similar implications but those that are more extensively explored in Shakespeare's oeuvre. That is, among the 'beautiful disassociated objects' to which the Renaissance beloved was compared were plants, namely flowers of all kinds. Plants are our focus here because in their cyclical lifespan, in their lived temporal materiality (against stone's much more epochal arc) they perform the dynamism that is then dramatically frozen in the fetishizing project of the poet. As Leah Knight acknowledges in her analysis of the Orpheus myth, plants are not inanimate.[17] While they cannot uproot themselves and walk (unless they are Birnam Wood), plants are not confined by the moment of their (human) idealization. They sprout, grow, bloom, seed, wither and replant (often in a place removed from where they previously did so). Shakespeare's texts in their engagement with material practice and our scholarly attention to historic specificity reveal both plants and women as changing, agentic and animate; nonetheless Petrarchism, in the comparison of plants to the beloved, holds both in a static space of prime bloom and optimal beauty. Perhaps the most notorious and salacious example is Edmund Spenser's *Amoretti* 64:

> Comming to kisse her lyps, (such grace I found)
> Me seemd I smelt a gardin of sweet flowres:
> That dainty odours from them threw around,
> For damzels fit to decke their lovers bowres.
> Her lips did smell lyke unto Gillyflowers,

> Her ruddy cheeks lyke unto Roses red:
> Her snowy browes lyke budded Bellamoures,
> Her lovely eyes lyke Pincks but newly spred,
> Her goodly bosome lyke a Strawberry bed,
> Her neck lyke to a bounch of Cullambynes:
> Her brest lyke lillyes, ere theyr leaves be shed,
> Her nipples lyke yong blossomd Jessemynes:
> Such fragrant flowres doe give most odorous smell,
> But her sweet odour did them all excell.[18]

In simply describing the scent of the beloved, Spenser assembles a garden that grows nowhere and at no one time, including a plant that remains an allusive fiction (the 'Bellamour'). One line in particular, 'Her breast lyke lillyes, ere theyr leaves be shed', encapsulates monumentalizing and thus fetishizing poeticization while providing a rhyming counterbalance to the 'Pincks but newly spred' (another blossom caught in one moment). In these lilies, we see the anxious workings of the blazon. For the idealized comparison to be effective, the bloom must stay within a set moment, in its most perfect state, and must not move through time into death (thus the pinks are differently-but-relatedly static). In the ecological psychology of Heft, this amounts to a thing divorced from its dynamism, and as soon as we articulate it as such, it is reified into less than itself. In suggesting the leaves will eventually be shed, however, the image reveals the tension related to maintaining its suspended state. In Petrarchan stasis, both beloved and that to which she is compared are seemingly no longer subject to the elements and to time's passage. Certainly, this is what poetic monumentalization in the sonnets intends, but in the ways that feminism has wanted to push at the denigration and abuse implicit in this imposed stasis, ecofeminism reminds us that this is multiply denigrating and abusive. The ideal imposed upon the beloved is also being imposed upon the plants. The lily is not allowed a dynamic move through time, nor is it permitted any malformations. Meanwhile, the plant's scent, the marker of its material presence upon which the poem depends, conveys the plant's ephemeral qualities – its seasonality – even as the poet seeks to keep these qualities at the margins.

Scholars need not look far to find evidence of this seasonality. If bereft of a comprehensive garden in the exact English climate, they can find a thorough accounting of the times of sowing, bloom, and harvesting of various plants in herbals and gardening manuals, but the manuscript archive also provides an immediate sense of a seasonal intimacy held by early moderns who delved in the earth and gathered from the fields. Whether it's Hugh Plat's vigilance in the unpredictable month of March discussed below, 'the imaginary of domestic preservation' discussed by Wendy Wall, or 'Elizabeth Downing's busy month of May' charted by Hillary Nunn,[19] there are many first-hand accounts of the human rhythms of labour, anxiety, and enjoyment that parallel the growth and death cycle of plants. In another example, a recipe called 'The Golden Oyle' found in a seventeenth-century collection at the Folger Shakespeare Library, the labour of one season anticipates that of the other. The grouping of the first three ingredients – violets, primroses, and cowslips – points to their springtime harvesting, unlike the rosemary and marigolds that follow as the recipe continues,

> Because all these hearbes are not to be had altogether, you must make use of such till you can gett the rest, stamp them as aforesaid, and infuse them in the Oyle, straining them everyday, to keepe them from moulding, till the Oile be made Compleate[.][20]

The process of steeping the plants in oil for later use may, on the surface, seem to be a material version of poetic monumentalization, but the movement through time from the violets and primroses to the rosemary and marigolds recognizes the practitioner's subjection to seasonal change. By comparison, in attempting to hold the plant in one moment of optimal bloom, the poet tries to ignore the dynamic back and forth of human and nonhuman that surrounds him.

The overt meaning of 'grace' in Spenser's first line – employed in a sense different than that applied to Hermione and stone above – may also appropriate from the plants their greater vitality. That is, two now obsolete senses of the word apply primarily to plants. One points to their medicinal powers, such as in the alternate name of rue as 'herb of grace';[21] the other references their pleasant odour.[22] While both may be read to apply in these lines as contingent meanings, as they come to pertain to the female love object, the dominant meaning of the word focuses on the adornment of her human presence.[23] In general, the separation (often gendered) of human and nonhuman in definitions of words despite their shared qualities provides consistent substance for analysis in ecofeminist enquiry. We see this in the ways that scientific discourse (discussed in Chapter 3) values codification of knowledge through language ('true' botany begins with Linnaeus' classification of plants) more than nonverbal experiential knowing (what is known through medical and culinary practice before Linnaeus). Thus linguistics, as the science of language, similarly looks to separate human and nonhuman in the development of language. Words that may at one point in their development apply to both humans and plants later have separate human and botanical definitions.

Shakespeare's characters reveal this yoking of human and nonhuman in the metaphoric constructions of language, which linguistic projects look to then untangle. Take, for example, the appearance of 'nip' when Saturninus hears of Lucius's growing power in *Titus Andronicus*:

Is warlike Lucius general of the Goths?
These tidings nip me and I hang the head
As flowers with frost or grass beat down with storms.
Ay, now begins our sorrows to approach.
'Tis he the common people love so much

(4.4.69–73)

Saturninus' imagery draws on experiences as recorded by gardeners such as Hugh Plat in his *Floraes Paradise* (1608) in an entry simply entitled 'Roses late':

> Cut your Roses when they are ready to bud in an apt time of the Moone, and they will begin to bud, when other roses haue done bearing: this is an excellent secret, if frosts happen in budding time: for so may you haue store of roses, when others shall haue fewe or none & may then be solde at a high rate. This I proued the 18. of March 1606, beeing a fewe daies after the change [of the moon], vpon diuers standerts at Bednall-greene [Suffolk], beeing *extreamelie nipped* with frosts, in budding time; & many of them did yeelde me great store of Roses, when the rest of my garden did in a manner faile.[24]

Plat's use refers directly to the meaning 'to check or destroy the growth of (a plant), as by the physical removal of a bud or the like, or through the action of cold or frost' (*OED*, 'nip', v., IV.13a), reflecting both human action and frost, but this definition is tied to the other meaning 'Of cold, frost ... injure or affect painfully', as seen in Edmund Spenser's line from the December eclogue, 'The carefull cold hath nypt my rugged rynde' (*OED*, 'nip', v., IV.11a). On one level, the inclusion of human suffering in this word-choice transfers onto the gardeners who lost their rose harvests in 1606. On another, as seen in Saturninus, this word implies a yoking together of human and plant in their subjugation. Saturninus' line also calls upon the old English meaning of 'niped', 'To bow the head; to bow down, bend, droop' (nipe, v.1), particularly before a sovereign, a definition that describes both those who hunch against cold winds and a rose blossom damaged by frost. Despite the material similarities of subjection, the *OED* separates out completely the older meaning from the botanical and frost associations; Shakespeare's texts reveal how they are tightly intertwined.

Thus for ecofeminism, which works against the division of human from nonhuman and looks for mutual implications,

Shakespeare's sonnets are doubly unconventional. Not only are the beloveds not idealized in a typical manner and the relationship itself is given to the fluctuations of time and societal elements,[25] but also the plants themselves are subject to the changing seasons and other factors. So by applying ecofeminist theory to the sonnets we can discover new and rich layers in Shakespeare's resistance to poetic conventions. We see this in the many cankers that populate the sequence that eat up roses 'to death' (Sonnet 99, l.12) and the festering lilies of Sonnet 94 (l.14). In making his plants the agents of active verbs – lilies fester, roses stand, violets steal – the poet re-energizes the comparison at the same time as he signifies the death of the relationship. Yes, he still confines the conception of the flowers for the sake of the comparison, but the comparison itself signifies a dynamic existence that defies this confinement. Attention to material practice also discloses the constant vigilance required in the maintenance of a garden, as Plat's *Floraes Paradise* contains clear instructions on how 'to destroy a canker'[26] as it does saving the rose from a frost. Whereas Spenser's 'ere theyr leaves be shed' hints at the tension behind monumentalization, Shakespeare's dead and dying blooms fully expose its vulnerable underbelly.

Again, as feminist readings have long considered the ways in which Shakespeare's heroines alongside those found in the pages of women writers in the period have challenged the silencing enacted in Petrarchism – speaking back, as it were, to the male sonneteer – plants themselves, in their dormant, dying, diseased, seeding, spreading selves confound any stasis imposed upon them. The only resistance the plants are seemingly given, as articulated within Shakespeare's sequence, however, is their deaths (sometimes untimely), which would make them more like Lucrece or Lavinia than Olivia or Pamphilia. The problem here – and this is paralleled by the limitations of a feminist analysis that only engages Shakespeare's words and not the extensive archive of women's lives that surrounds them – is that plants, like women, live outside the texts and are not dependent on these texts for their existence.

Thus ecofeminism looks at actual plants and material practices with plants to gain a better sense of this dynamism. In the way that the baker knows dough better than the psychologist knows dough,[27] the ecofeminist combs through gardening manuals and recipe books as well as the garden itself for indications of resistance to a static human–plant relation and thus finds one that is more dynamic. If we think of the plants in just such a material context, the garden of Shakespeare's Sonnet 99 comes alive as each plant listed blooms in sequential order; violets precede lilies, which come before marjoram as can be seen when we consult herbals or seasonal timelines often found in recipe books,[28] and so Spenser's 'gardin of sweet flowres' clearly reveals itself as fantasy, as no such garden can exist with all of these blooms occupying one space (not to mention the Bellamours).[29] Looking at specific plants, Ophelia's herbs similarly defy the reading of love token or even sweet-scented herbs to lay upon a tomb, as rue is 'rank-smelling'. It is not known for its flowers but rather for its foul-tasting-but-potent medicinal qualities, as seen in a repeated plague recipe that shrouds the leaves of the plant in the sweetness of dried fruit, such as this one found in a mid-seventeenth-century collection held at Bryn Mawr: 'Take Rue and the kernell of a Wallnutt and Bay salt and putt it in a Figg and eate it fasting' or another that uses raisins instead of figs found in a letter written by Maria Thynne to her husband in London.[30] The plants do not live solely for their would-be authors' benefits, and real plants may reveal the limits of the conceptualization of them. In this light, the stasis of the blazon tradition undoes itself, as the objectifying catalogue denies the actuated dynamism, the inner light and the absence thereof, that brought us to the garden and the beloved in the first place.

This emphasis on seasonal/epochal/cyclical dynamism, existence through time, is why the materialism of ecofeminism is different than the cultural materialism of Natasha Korda, but it is related in the way that her analysis sparkles in its articulation of the context of material production.[31] That is, often what precedes the intimate knowing we describe is the act of labour, an engaging material practice that is not about mere consumption. Unlike cultural materialism, however, the materials of ecofeminism are the things that exist despite us, the raw materials – the creatures and the natural resources – that become the bangles, the food, the clothes and the medicine that may sustain and adorn human existence. These materials are also, by implication, the very material beings, human and nonhuman, that are affected by our existence, often without our knowing. An ecofeminist reading serves as an alternative to those that would speak for nature and women, those that are philosophically speculative, and others that call upon the Aristotelian depiction of vegetable nature (and women-as-vegetable-matter) as the lesser part of humanity, those that relegate the question firmly within the history of ideas. Instead, ecofeminism considers the symbiotic interrelation of things that grow, human and nonhuman, while considering how these relations are often figured in pointedly gendered terms.[32]

(Boys as) women as plants

Shakespeare's plays present another form of plant resistance (other than their deaths and their unpleasant odours), one that an ecofeminist approach to his oeuvre here strives both to articulate and problematize. That is, Shakespeare embodies plants through several of his characters and in doing so reintroduces a kind of dynamism to the conceptualization of these plants in their symbolic or simply metaphoric values. This discussion is related to the analysis of the alignment of young women such as Ophelia, Marina and Perdita with the flowers they carry as virginal Persephones, preambles or alternatives to the fall. Also related is the more extensive archival work conducted by Hillary Nunn on greensickness and 'vegetating virgins'[33] that shows this association between flowers and virgins in medical and dramatic discourse.

As in the sonnet tradition, which we discussed earlier, Shakespeare's female characters frequently figure as plants, evoking the metaphorical connection between them and the familiar move in the period's literature that has oft been discussed as objectifying and degrading. However, as we see in *All's Well That Ends Well*, female characters in Shakespeare also actively employ this link between themselves and plants in such a way that more overtly highlights their mutual embeddedness as co-agentic. In this way, both women and plants simultaneously become subject and object, an and/both relation that is empowering in its ability to resist subjection by a dominant (male) Other. After having just defended Helena's position in the Countess's family, whereby Helena both is 'bequeath'd' to the Countess by her father (a commodity traded from one family to the next) and her own woman (able 'lawfully /[to] make title to as much love as she finds'), the Countess seizes upon what is perhaps the most common metaphor for women in the period: woman-as-rose (1.3. 100–101). But here, both Helena and the Countess are not roses to be possessed by a male lover; their link to 'nature' is instead further illustration of their agency and independence:

> If ever we are nature's, these are ours; this thorn
> Doth to our rose of youth rightly belong;
> Our blood to us, this to our blood is born:
> It is the show and seal of nature's truth,
> Where love's strong passion is impress'd in youth.
>
> (1.3.126–30)

The 'seal of nature's truth', hardly proof of women's inferiority, is instead evidence of their ability to choose for themselves, to act upon 'love's strong passion' rather than to be acted upon. Such self-determination in this passage is tied to the reciprocal language by which women and 'nature' are intertwined: they are 'nature's' and the things of nature are they; the 'blood' within them mingles with the blood drawn by the rose's thorn. Diana uses similar language later in the play to chastise Bertram for using women as objects. She says, 'Ay, so you serve us / Till we serve you; but when you have our roses, / You barely leave our thorns to prick ourselves' (4.2.17–19). Like the Countess, Diana reclaims the metaphor and repositions women and plants not as objects but as subjects in their own right. Men may appear to take women's 'roses' and leave them only with 'thorns', but both women and thorns assume an active role in their own pricking, a phrase suggestive of their satisfying themselves by way of a reclamation of the phallic 'prick' that would seem to lie only in the hands of men. Women's desire here is hardly subject to men's; and they are hardly the object of men's desire or objects to be had.

Such seizure of the woman/nature metaphor also serves to undermine the gender/class structure that scholars have pointed out lies in peril in the play. Jean Howard argues, for example, that what appears to be female agency in the play in fact serves patriarchal imperatives.[34] However, it is the link between woman and plant, so commonly used to undermine women's authority in the period, that here instead exposes the limits of such a system. Grafting of woman to woman, rather than heterosexual coupling within a patrilineal system, serves as the means by which the Countess claims Helena as her own; the relationship between the two women, and the two women-as-trees, thus becomes a sort of matrilineal realignment catalysed by the Countess and a means of social mobility for Helena. Erin Ellerbeck has discussed the horticultural language in this scene in particular as 'blurring the boundaries of biological and adoptive parent–child relations' but concludes that such language employed by the Countess positions her in competition with nature.[35] For Ellerbeck, the play makes a distinction between the choice of foster parents and 'natural' childbirth. However, this notion of 'natural', albeit conforming to the dominant ideas of the period, itself ultimately reifies dominant ideas and the human/nonhuman binary. Instead, we argue, this botanical language operates as a way to trouble the natural/artificial *and* human/nonhuman binaries, the way women draw on their connection to the nonhuman world elsewhere in the play (as roses, thorns, etc.) and the horticultural language in this scene serve as the means by which women articulate and act upon their own desire. We might recall, of course, that the Countess begins her grafting speech with 'I say I am your mother, / And put you in the catalogue of those / That were enwombed mine', making her assertion of this adoptive mother-child bond as legitimate as the biological process of pregnancy (1.3.139–41). And so it seems especially significant that she follows this claim to legitimacy through her desire and her womb, conspicuously omitting a male contribution, with the grafting language, whereby "Tis often seen / Adoption strives with nature, and choice breeds / A native slip to us from foreign seeds' (1.3.141–3). The grafting of the 'native slip ... from foreign seeds' is bred, like Helena to the Countess's womb, by 'choice', where such choice and 'nature' are not at odds but rather in sync. The 'native' and the 'foreign' become one in the same through the graft much as Helena becomes the equivalent of the Countess's biological child. What is artificial is also natural such that desire and choice are not only human qualities, then, but are also 'natural' and exemplify the connection between humans and nonhumans – here, women and plants.

For what remains of this chapter, however, rather than focus on the language of comparison or proximity inherent to *women*-as-plants, we consider how Shakespearean actors, because *neither* women *nor* plant, enact flower personae *at the same time* as they perform female human characters, and in doing so destabilize the notion that either woman or plant is a static entity. Most notably, for the purposes of this analysis of the sonnet tradition, we present Viola and Rosalind. Here we show how, for Shakespeare, that which is often constructed as inanimate is animate indeed, as women and nonhuman nature are active, co-creative subjects, not passive objects for male (and 'human' as an extension of dominant male) consumption. Viola and Rosalind at first seem to highlight the fragrant and idealized beauty of these women. From the opening speech of

Twelfth Night that compares music to 'the sweet sound / That breathes upon a bank of violets, / Stealing and giving odour' (1.1.5–7), violets are in the air of *Twelfth Night*. The character with the more general floral name of Viola (a name that will not be uttered until the final act) arrives in the first lines of the next scene. It is as if the scent and its music have come to earth in female form. Unlike Viola's, we know Rosalind's name from the first moment we meet her in Act 1, scene 2 of *As You Like It*, and her name resonates with the tradition before it, from Romeo's first love to Colin Clout's one and true. But it is later in that same scene that she becomes identified with the rose, when we discover her cousin's nickname for her, Celia calling her 'my sweet Rose, my dear Rose' (1.2.21–2). This conflagration of beloved with rose resonates with Shakespeare's sonnet sequence, as throughout he refers to the male beloved as 'beauty's rose' (Sonnet 1, l.2) and 'my rose' (Sonnet 109, l.14), and this image is then made physical, in the sonnets, in real roses that are killed by cankers (Sonnet 99, l.12) and in *As You Like It* by the presence of the boy actor. Thus on the surface level, we may read these as personifications and as an extension of the tradition. The violet signifying spring and sweetness paints this character as a youthful ideal. Through the naming of the rose, we know Rosalind's beauty beyond the actor's physical attributes.

This understanding is a limited one, however, that depends on the conception of beauty aligned with the plants. Not only are both characters imbued with botanical healing properties that ease melancholy and cool choler, but also Viola and Rosalind speak against the stasis imposed by the sonnet tradition as breathing exempla of the image come alive. In being named for two of the central flowers in the blazon tradition, they ask us to consider what it means to compare a woman to a flower, that is, to compare her to that which withers and dies and is reborn again to its perfection. At key moments, both plays invoke this life cycle with relation to the plant and in doing so complicate the comparison inherent in the name. Just as 'women' in these lines is a generalized category being observed, the lines in question are not 'the violet's' or 'the rose's' but rather the more generic 'Plant's' as presented through a dramatic mask. In naming Viola and Rose, the playwright invokes the tradition of stasis at the same time as he presents the dynamic alternative to it. In speaking against the abstracted beauty foisted upon feeling and complex humans, Rosalind and Viola as female characters also representing plants challenge the conception of the garden that keeps it in an unrealizable static perfection.

Most pointedly, Viola and Rosalind raise their challenges while dressed as Cesario and Ganymede, and such cross-dressing has been a subject of much feminist scholarly discussion as discussed by Phyllis Rackin and others.[36] In cross-dressing, these characters 'call attention' to gender as it is being performed, and in so doing reveal how gender is performance. At this moment, it may be useful to remember our allegory in that, during the statue scene in its early modern performance, the stone statue that is imbued with a feminine spirit by Leontes is actually embodied by a boy actor, that is, the body in performance is neither of the entities, woman or statue, that it seems to be, thus placing women and statue in the position of 'being represented' in an overt way. But through an ecofeminist lens this cross-dressing has multiple implications. Not only is the male actor presenting the position of the female character playing a young man, but also the human male actor is presenting the plant position through the human female character playing a young man. This layering of performances and multiplicity of being again emphasize the various ways in which one may read the lines iterated. In the way that feminist criticism may read 'the capacity of cross-dressed performance' 'to destabilize the gender norms of the represented action' through feminist analysis,[37] ecofeminist enquiry views plant personification as a kind of cross-species impersonation in which the speciesist voicing is attenuated and interrupted by a multi-layered embodiment such that the notion of animate/inanimate, human/nonhuman, subject/object is shown to be elusive, untenable.

The first of these occurrences is most overt, as it invokes a flower as physical ideal and thus the sonnet tradition directly. Orsino and Viola/Cesario speak about the superficial nature of men's love:

> ORSINO ... Let still the woman take
> An elder than herself; so wears she to him,
> So sways she level in her husband's heart:
> For boy, however we do praise ourselves,
> Our fancies are more giddy and unfirm,
> More longing, wavering, sooner lost and worn,
> Than women's are.
>
> VIOLA   I think it well, my lord.
>
> ORSINO Then let thy love be younger than thyself,
> Or thy affection cannot hold the bent:
> For women are as roses, whose fair flower
> Being once display'd, doth fall that very hour.
>
> VIOLA And so they are: alas, that they are so:
> To die, even when they to perfection grow!
>
> (2.4.29–41)

Orsino's honest acknowledgement of the 'unfirm' quality of a love that requires the female beloved to remain at the height of beauty is seemingly reiterated by seeming-Cesario's concession. But the character *Viola*'s repetition of his sentiment, given her position as both flower and woman, contains deep irony. That is, Viola's 'they' here really should be read as 'we', and in the collective 'we' – of women, of plants and of women-as-plants – Viola exposes the true 'we' of the shared mortality of all on the stage. Orsino and Cesario/Viola are both 'as roses', ever dying. This pronoun slippage coming from Cesario would seem to remove Orsino and Cesario from women and plants, but Viola's dual position as woman and plant undermines that removal and thus transforms 'they' into 'we'.

Hence, an important difference between how we understand these moments in Shakespeare and how Posthumanist or OOO theorists might understand them is the emphasis on the imaginative fiction they create, one that defies isolating the human from nonhuman and instead shows them to be woven together inextricably. This is not a matter of speaking for plants any more than Viola speaks for women, but in creating a speaking position through which both plants and women may be 'heard', Shakespeare's texts interrupt the (dominant male) narrative that objectifies and silences in its very conception. In doing so, the play releases the dynamic object from its objectification. Such a reading exemplifies what Val Plumwood calls 'thinking differently', one that steps outside of human/nonhuman dualism and imagines an 'active voice' for all that exists in the world.[38] This understanding is key to how ecofeminist analysis differs (and builds on) both feminist and ecocritical work: that unless we think differently to locate an 'active voice' for all, we are ultimately still reinforcing categories of subject/object. So, feminists might look for ways to reorient the male/female binary, but unless we get at the concomitant binary of human/nonhuman, with which the other is aligned, we reify both.

In this way of thinking, we may also re-read Rosalind's counterfeit misogyny as voiced by Ganymede when speaking of Orlando's love for Rosalind (who Orlando imagines to be absent).

ROSALIND Now tell me how long you would have her [i.e. Rosalind], after you have possessed her?

ORLANDO For ever, and a day.

ROSALIND Say a day, without the ever. No, no, Orlando, men are April when they woo, December when they wed. Maids are May when they are maids, but the sky changes when they are wives. I will be more jealous of thee than a Barbary cock-pigeon over his hen, more clamorous than a parrot against rain, more new-fangled than an ape, more giddy in my desires than a monkey.

(4.1.136–46)

Orlando's desire for an immortal love here is similar to the displacement voiced by Duke Orsino (only women and roses are mortal), but it differs in Orlando's youth. Orsino, a bit more jaded, recognizes his own fickleness and that of men, while Orlando, newly and first time in love with his Rosalind (not unlike Romeo before him), cannot imagine another. Rosalind/Ganymede not only points out the changeability of affection, but also notes the capriciousness of human beings. While she articulates these vicissitudes through a virtual menagerie, her opening catalogue of months particularly resounds if we read this as a moment of plant impersonation. The April and May of the wooer and maids respectively are juxtaposed to the December and changing skies of less agreeable seasons. Read as spoken by a human, Rosalind seems to be speaking of the life cycle, the May–December romance perhaps; in this interpretation, in the April of their youths, men occupy the position of wooer severally, only marrying when they enter the last phase of life, and the women they marry alter once wed. But read more closely, this is not what Rose is saying; read as spoken by a plant, this can only mean the weather. April and May being a time of new plants and new beginnings, it is the season of the bloom in newest bud, but in marriage, the weather changes, the bloom fades, the love becomes tempestuous. The seasonal narrative here underlines the shared position of love, women, men, and plants. No longer held in a vernal apex but imagined in winter, love dies with the rest of us. While this reading may be true even if plant-personification was not in play, the 'rose' behind the delivery of Rosalind's lines converts the notion that women's changeability is a negative (because it makes them out of control) and makes it a source of power – women's power and plants'. In withering, plants release their seeds; in their 'infinite variety', women are more than the conventional conception of them. That is, the point of seeming plant personification is not simply to point out to young lovers that they and their loves will die. It is, rather, to place both plants and humans back in the cycle of dust to dust, to undo the monumentalizing motifs of the sonnet tradition – held in perfection 'for ever and a day' – and to acknowledge the dynamism of that which has hitherto been objectified. At this moment, we are reminded of the wrinkles that have defied the 'unchangeable' nature of Hermione's idealized memorialization. We are reminded of the power that time has given both her and Paulina. In this acknowledgement, new paradigms emerge, ones that are more closely aligned with the thing itself rather than the fear of mortality projected onto it. To discover these post-sonnet potentials more fully articulated in Shakespeare's later works, we now turn back to *The Winter's Tale*.

While Hermione and Leontes are afflicted by unrealizable ideals and extreme reactions when they are inevitably not fulfilled, the next generation, occupying a different environment altogether, calls upon plants as distinctive and realizable exempla. Unencumbered by the conventions of court, Perdita employs her botanical knowledge learned as a shepherd's daughter and emphasizes the human–plant connection.[39] In this active and immediate relationship, her plants are not only beautiful, but also susceptible to the fluctuations inherent to changing seasons. Most telling is her depiction of the daffodil. In Perdita's poetry, the daffodil's ability to withstand seasonal adversity is central, the beauty an extension of its hardiness: 'daffodils, / That come before the swallow dares, and take / The winds of March with beauty;' (4.4.118–20). Her lines importantly do anthropomorphize the plants (along with the swallows) in describing the daffodils' bearing as courageous against the 'winds', both literal (being colder) and figurative (being changeable weather), that March brings. This passage also anthropomorphizes with the use of 'take' in which the daffodils take the air that is the March winds (III.13b),[40] 'suffer' the 'physical blows' that are the March winds (VI.35), or 'submit to' the troubles that March may bring (VI.34b).⁴¹ 'With beauty' opens up a fourth possibility in a more symbiotic relationship between daffodils and vicissitudes in that its hardy position in March contributes to its beautiful aspect, calling upon the meaning of 'take' that is 'to accept without objection, opposition, or resentment' (VI.42b), as the wind becomes part of the daffodil's Buddhistic state of being. Again, however, in identifying the plants with human characteristics she is not projecting humanity onto them but is rather making an argument to Florizel (perhaps the embodiment of all flowers – 'Florae's all') that he must be as the daffodil in not knowing how his father will respond to the news of their love. Florizel adopts her philosophy; later, after his father rages with threats of 'dead blow[s]' (4.4.436), he describes himself and Perdita as 'flies / Of every wind that blows' (4.4.542–3). Again, this is not speaking for plants, but in being with and of plants, Perdita and Florizel internalize their virtues in a material way, not unlike the taking of medicine. It is important to remind ourselves throughout this consideration that most early moderns perceived the ingesting of plants as physically changing the body from one humour to another. For example, syrup of violets, a cold and moist plant, was taken to alleviate fevers or to cause drowsiness. If we compare this internalization of plant matter with the more tragic version – in which Juliet imbibes a plant substance of which neither she nor the audience knows the name – Perdita and Florizel name and know the qualities of plants, and in so doing find a kind of remedy, one that draws on botanical potency, to what could be a calamitous situation. In this way, Perdita and her daffodils demonstrate an alternative to reducing women and nonhumans to simple 'love objects' derived from the Petrarchan discursive tradition, 'things of pleasure' that stem from misogynist and consumerist denigration, or culturally exotic, reduced essences or caricatures obtainable and distillable by way of orientalist discourse or colonial practice. In her identification with the seemingly inanimate thing, she recognizes its life more fully and at the same time adds meaning to her own. For her, the daffodil exists on its own terms and in its own time, and its beauty is most manifest in its dynamic, flexible, relationship to its context.

Petrarch in the produce aisle

We might well employ such sympathetic identification, emphasizing dynamism over stasis, as a way to redress the conception of a nature held in perfection indefinitely and suspended out of context that has undone us today. The deep-rooted Petrarchan standards that equate youth/freshness/flawlessness with beauty for both women and plants has led to the exploitation of natural resources in Europe and the US to serve modes of production that deplete the health of populations and compromise rather than enhance the quality of life for both humans and nonhumans. The cosmetic industry subjects animals to horrific testing, old growth forests to clear cutting for palm and other oils, and its consumers to damaging chemicals, all in the name of idealized beauty. Divorced from plants and animals in any other than a commoditized context, US consumers in particular are trapped in an inflexible and destructive paradigm, one that is prone to fetishization and degradation.

The need to buy fruit and vegetables at their superficially optimal state, unbruised and unblemished, for instance, means that we have bred them to last but not have taste, fragrance or the robustness they can only achieve when they ripen naturally. The sweet strawberries from Spenser's poem ironically have become practically inaccessible to modern US consumers disconnected from heirloom strawberry fields *because of* the very idealization that the poem exemplifies.[42] Similarly, tons of food representing hours of labour (often indentured and slave-wage labour by workers who have few rights and even less recourse to rectify their situation) and gallons of valuable water and other resources are discarded at the Mexican border as they fail to meet US consumer standards. The entanglement with poorly paid and exploited labour throughout agricultural history again underscores how we cannot divorce sociological issues from environmental ones: when the nonhuman environment is reduced to its base utility, so are humans. And this idealizing aesthetic that has compromised our food cycle is related to the same one that has held up women (and continues to do so) against an unrealizable model, as recent work on 'body shaming' illustrates.[43]

It may be irony or a cosmic corrective that a place of the origin of the poetic ideals, France, the land of the troubadours, is one of the first European countries to 'lead the way' in remedying the ills in the food marketplace.[44] In making it illegal for grocers to discard food that is edible, the French government has intervened in a centuries-old aesthetic and redefined what is desirable. The campaign began with a single grocery chain that chose to sell 'ugly' – a partly-anthropomorphizing adjective that shows the alignment of vegetable and human physical ideals – vegetables.[45] In the US, non-profit start-ups have followed suit, selling 'ageing food' or vegetables 'past their prime' (again, descriptors that connote humans in the winter of their lives being shuffled off centre stage) at affordable prices.[46] One can even have such 'imperfect' food delivered to your front porch.[47] These programmes provide a green anti-blazon to the brightly lit and newly spritzed archetype fetishized through high-end supermarkets. In a world where millions are hungry and soil and water are increasingly scarce, it is especially despicable that in 2014 we wasted approximately one-third of the food produced.[48] France, following a European Union pledge to reduce food waste by 50 per cent in one decade, along with US grass-roots organizations, has asked us to look again, to examine what it is we value, and, by implication, devalue, in the wider culture. That one of the most high-profile examples of a US chain that will sell 'ugly' vegetables is Whole Foods,[49] with its reputation for a more affluent and hipster clientele, may make this movement arguably problematic as it reassigns desire; so too might the fact that the 'ugly' remnants are given to charity or to animal feedlots and 'ageing food' is sold in 'low-to-middle income ... neighborhoods' reassert sociological hierarchies, a fact that should be examined in itself. But in these cases, these vegetable detritus are at least not discarded or dismissed as if not worthy of use or attention – they are no longer understood as 'waste'.

The road from Petrarchan lilies captured in the moment before their petals wilt to cardboard strawberries and November asparagus is one built on the commodification of the ideal and the denigration of those locked out of the possible attainment of that ideal for whatever genetic, ethnic, socioeconomic, meteorological, temporal or accidental reason. An ecofeminist approach demonstrates the complete entanglement of human and nonhuman abuse while making overt the implications, the imperilment of both abused and abuser, that result. Through this lens, poetic and linguistic convention may be seen to have material, sociological consequences. In such readings, Shakespeare's female characters are the very earth, trees, flowers, animals and stones, as are his male characters,[50] as are we all.

Conclusion: Nature, stir: Ecofeminists in the archive

Strike all that look upon you with marvel. Come!
I'll fill your grave up: stir, nay, come away:
Bequeath to death your numbness; for from him
Dear life redeems you.[1]

[W]hen this hearbe should be gathered, touch not the hearbe it selfe with your hands, for then the uertue thereof is gone yee must gathere & plucke it out of the ground by the stalke yee must lay it in a cleane basket the leaues of it is full of strenght [sic] & nature.[2]

The world we have lost was organic.[3]

Healing nature

We begin this final chapter by revisiting Carolyn Merchant's analysis of the 'death of nature', the result of the discourses and practices of the scientific revolution, colonial expansion and industrialization. Indeed, her study begins with a call to 're-evaluate' 'the contributions of such founding "fathers" of modern science as Francis Bacon, William Harvey, René Descartes, Thomas Hobbes, and Isaac Newton',[4] and almost forty years later these contributions have duly been dissected and problematized, increasingly so as climate change has become – for most, at least – an acknowledged reality. Four decades later, moreover, we have come to see that these contributions are but part of the story, albeit a powerful, dominating, destructive part.

Underneath the processes of scientific objectification, colonial domination and industrial commercialization can be found the counter discourses of material intimacy, indigenous knowledge practices and alternative economies that provide another mode of being, one resistant to depersonalizing changes. In the exchange of medical recipes among lay practitioners we can see all of these at play, as immediate and local expertise of ingredients combine with non-monetary exchange and bartering. We see this in Shakespeare's servant characters, who, as in *Romeo and Juliet* and *Twelfth Night*, call out for 'aqua vitae' or the wisewoman in the face of duress or madness, or in *All's Well*'s Helena, who negotiates with the king without ever asking outright for payment. These characters exist against the practice of the elite, who call in the physicians, or that of the physicians themselves, who live on retainer. Within the polyvocality of his texts, we can find voices that exist despite, perhaps because of, those that overshadow or even control them.

That is, Merchant's interrogation of the dominant voices of the Enlightenment has done much to de-centre and render uncertain the foundations of current economies and scientific practice at the same time as it has also opened a space for alternatives to be rediscovered and otherwise to gain the spotlight. As an early modern literary historical example, Sylvia Bowerbank's *Speaking for Nature: Women and Ecologies of Early Modern England* shifts from violent metaphors of the male proto-scientists' rape and murder of nature to that of courtship and marriage. And arguably, following Merchant's discussion of Anne Conway's vitalism at the end of *Death of Nature*, Bowerbank's turn reflects her focus to only female authors and readers who are subject to Baconian paradigms but resistant to and resilient in the face of dominant ideas. In analysing our contemporary moment, Vandana Shiva's *Staying Alive*, its introduction heavily dependent on Merchant's relation of Baconian natural history to colonial expansion, as the indigenous practices that defy its foundation become increasingly endangered by it. As feminist criticism has done in parallel, ecofeminist analysis has searched for alternatives to the destructive paradigm against which it first raised its voice. In these alternatives lie the seeds of resistance and resilience. Within Shakespearean ecocriticism, the authority of elite male voices such as Francis Bacon and Gervase Markham has skewed how we have come to see the ways the early moderns related to the environment. Through the many voices of Shakespeare's plays, however, our analysis has strived to bring to the forefront other perspectives, those of labourers, women, the poor and the enslaved, but the discovery of these largely textually illiterate viewpoints in the record takes some digging.

In digging, we discover that Nature did not, indeed, die with the industrial scientific complex, but it did take a beating. The Renaissance view 'that all things were permeated by life, there being no adequate method by which to designate the inanimate from the animate' persisted in material practices dependent on an intimate relationship to those things.[5] In that intimacy is felt loss, and in it is also found endurance. As individuals are identified with the things of nature, they also understand at a deep level the implications of those things' destruction. Thus the postcolonial identification with Caliban is not simply about the subjected character, but also about his intimacy with the world around him: his lack of fear in hearing the 'sounds, and sweet airs, that give delight and hurt not' of the island as well as his deep sense of loss felt in waking to a world of enslavement.[6] By the means that the enslaved, the objectified and the exploited have resisted and organized, nature has not died, though she, and we call upon Lynne Bruckner's defence of that pronoun, certainly has, as Merchant posits, been 'threatened', and with increasing ferocity.[7]

In the introductory chapter of this book, we illustrate how much of twenty-first-century ecofeminism has focused on the interconnection, the enmeshment, with the material world that is human existence. These theories go further than what Merchant termed 'the dialectical relationship between human behavior and institutions ... and the natural environment'.[8] But an essential difference for us as well as for Merchant is our shared 'focus' 'on early modern Europe as an ecosystem', a focus that 'means more than discovering that today's kind of environmental crisis has occurred in the past'.[9] Merchant calls for 'a special sensitivity' to the dialectical relationship, and here we call for that sensitivity to be applied to human enmeshment with the nonhuman world. While Merchant thus looks for broad arcs of history – peasant revolts and the rise of capitalism – we instead turn to medicinal recipes, cosy fires and dying flowers. This turn to the intimate is not an escape to minutiae, the fetishization of things, as some have argued, but rather a search for local resistance to the grand narrative of the rise of the market economy, evidence of the persistent practice of intimate relations with the environment, and the resulting awareness of our mutual vulnerabilities and resiliencies.[10] It asserts, as Bruckner so beautifully explores, 'the importance of regarding humans as part of and intimately connected to N/nature'[11] in ways that a broad survey of the ideological underpinnings of our mutual large-scale destruction, such as deforestation or industrialization, may not.

As reflected in the previous chapters, an overt and fruitful record of such intimate connections can be found in the manuscript recipe books of the period. Recipe books can help us to articulate 'an ecosystem model' that 'reveals the limits of demographic, economic or political factors as single underlying explanations of history' and the immediate ways that 'disruption of associative ecosystems' affect 'human health, nutrition, and welfare'.[12] Recipe books aid in the recovery of the sort of 'ecosystem model' Merchant proposes as we move from the global to the local, as they say, to focus on *smaller-scale practices*, or what Rosi Braidotti terms 'micro-practices' that recall a mutual sense of 'sustainable becoming'. It is in such 'micro-practices' that we might look to locate models of 'the ethical state of becoming [that] practices a humble kind of hope, rooted in the ordinary micro-practices of everyday life'.[13] Considering such 'micro-practices' helps us account for how

> the material self cannot be disentangled from networks that are simultaneously economic, political, cultural, scientific, and substantial such that what was once the ostensibly bounded human subject enters a swirling landscape of uncertainty where practice and actions that were once not even remotely ethical or political matters suddenly become the very stuff of the crises at hand.[14]

To assert that 'early moderns' had particular attitudes about sustainable practices demonstrated by, say, deforestation or air pollution – in particular, how such attitudes manifested a view of the nonhuman world as a commodity at the service of (early) capitalist exchange – is quite different from an examination of how the everyday work in the household suggested human–nonhuman relations dependent on rather un-sentimentalized subsistence economies.

And so it is in this search for the small, the local, the 'micro-practices', that we see promise in a turn to early modern household cookery and medicine. In the early seventeenth-century manuscript recipe book of Lady Frances Catchmay, for instance, we see the interplay between human hand, cloth, cooking pot, herb, dirt and water contingent on interaction with and consumption of nonhuman things not for the purposes of capitalist accumulation but household (and bodily) harmony. They express and enact the very principles of sustainable relations that we propose to recuperate; their details recount an intra-action between an embeddedness of human and nonhuman things that renders inscrutable the line between one and the other. These recipes and their particulars put into relief a focus on practices writ large on the landscape (such as deforestation), and they show how environmental histories look quite different when we focus instead on practices writ small (or smaller) on the body, on the household, on its more immediate environs. Instead of severed connections, we find embedded experience and practices, entanglements of the sort described by Stacy Alaimo, Karen Barad, Val Plumwood and Donna Haraway.[15] As such, manuscript recipe books provide not only a rich, but also a requisite alternative narrative that demonstrates 'a way of reckoning with and welcoming the perpetual openness of complex chaotic systems to unexpected new judgments and configurations', described by Jeremy Davies as a way 'to reformulate [sustainability] in a way that attends to the problematic implications of its desire for permanence'.[16]

In 'A good Receyte to make matheglin', about a third of the way through Catchmay's book, the person preparing the drink is instructed to 'gather ... around michelmas or lammas' an assortment of herbs: fumitory, fennel, rosemary, hyssop, chamomile, thyme, marigolds, ribwort, parsley, selfheal and others. And then we get the following instruction: 'When you haue gathered thes hearbs and roots, make them very cleane that no earth be lefte vpon them.'[17] To use the term 'earth' begs a different way of thinking about the relationship between human and nonhuman things here. This recipe expresses an intimacy between the person who gathers, slices, boils the plants – articulated, for instance, in the reminder to 'haue care to slitt the ffenell roots and take out the harts stringe which groweth in the middest' – in water, over fire whose temperature (in all likelihood) she aims to regulate during the process. But what does it mean that she would remove earth from the herbs, clean them so that 'no earth be left vpon them'? Is this a disavowal of the unity of plant and earth, between the material growing and material grown? Or does the touching of earth by water and human hands, even if to remove it, simply express a different aspect of this intimacy?

This recipe, like so many others, punctuates inextricable points of contact between human and nonhuman that are key to thinking about their relationship differently. If we understand this contact only insofar as it enables separation – the slicing to sever leaf from stem of herb, the cleaning to remove earth – then perhaps we are simply reproducing the same distinction of dirt and soil that troubles much of our public discourse and undergirds a sense of human/nonhuman distinction.[18] That is, to see dirt as that thing that is necessarily not part of 'us', as that which exists apart from the human world, would presume that nonhuman things are inherently not 'human'. Removing earth from plant might seem to evoke this. But to have 'no earth left vpon them' is only possible by way of the tactile contact between human and nonhuman entity; and may it not perhaps suggest that 'earth' is not gone but rather part of another (or multiple) thing/s and that it is intrinsically linked with the human? If the cleaning process uses water, then the 'earth' mingles with water; or if the cleaning amounts to brushing the earth from plant with the hand, then hand and earth mix, earth falls perhaps back to, well, earth. What if, that is, the process of cleaning and removing earth, as described here, details not a severing of human and nonhuman thing but rather an ever-intimate reciprocal and symbiotic relationship bound by circular comings and goings and not teleological notions of here and gone? After all, that same earth will be the medium from which the woman harvests new herbs in the future, the surface upon which she walks to locate the herbs and do said gathering, as she repeats this and other recipes in the course of her domestic labour. And so, to understand 'earth' in this recipe as we do 'dirt' today – as in, when we throw away that piece of cake that touches the floor because it is 'dirty' – seems at odds with the task the early modern woman would have undertaken. Rather, it seems that this recipe, in its evocation of 'earth', suggests instead a process of something more akin to what we would think of as a sustainable and perpetual (re)turn of material to material, of intimate connections between human and nonhuman, whether that nonhuman thing is plant, element (fire, water) or 'earth'.

Catchmay's book prescribes a similar combination of harvesting, medicine preparation and administration in 'A very good medicen for eyes that be trobled with a pinne and webbe or with any other dymnes.'[19] In it, the person preparing the concoction is instructed to

> Take the oyle of a newe layd egge or two, beate and clapp it well till it come to afrothe, then let it stande so a little while, and let the oyle Runne into a saucer, and put the Iuce of daysies, with the blossomes, leaves and rootes, beinge stamped and strayned into the oyle of the egges, put alittle clarified honey to it and mixt all thes together well, and let the patient take every eveninge and morninge into his Eye that is greaved adroppe put in with a fether, let this be vsed so longe as he hathe payne.[20]

As with the first recipe we discussed, we see here a medicine intended for preservation and later use; however, its creation and efficacy depend not on discrete human/nonhuman entities but rather the intimate 'micro-practices' that constitute human–nonhuman assemblages. The person preparing the remedy uses a 'new layd egge or two', which means that the cure depends on the immediacy of time, participation (at least tacit) by the chickens who produce said egg/s, and human movement across ground, into henhouse to gather it. And how 'new' is a 'new layd egge'? Is it still warm? Can it be several hours or even days old? To know what constitutes 'new layd' to prepare the cure requires the housewife (in all likelihood) to have such intimate knowledge of egg and chicken – touching the warmth of the egg newly delivered, observing the point at which eggs go bad and are no longer fresh enough to be efficacious – of past, present and future converging; 'new layd' marks an act that has happened (the chicken laid the egg), the egg 'beate[n]' and 'clappe[d]' to incorporate egg matter, mixing bowl and human energy to create the new substance, the resulting 'frothe'. And to 'put the Iuce of daysies, with the blossomes, leaves and rootes, beinge stamped and strayned into the oyle of the egges' not only synthesizes said egg–bowl–human mixture with plant matter, but it depends on a recent human harvest of daisies, which is the result of human form crossing household threshold into adjoining environs (immediate or further afield) to pick fresh daisies so that they might still have juice to be strained. And again, as human feet traverse the dirt- or gravel-covered pathways outside, sights and sounds of nonhuman activity penetrate human bodily boundaries – a wooden stamper encircled by human hands 'stampe[s] and strayne[s]' the various parts of the daisies, daisy juice (roots, leaves, and all) and mingles with frothy oil of egg mixture. Here are things in perpetual flux, immediacy and futurity intertwined.

This recipe illustrates how humans and nonhumans are bound to one another in yet other ways too. The clarified honey added to the plant–egg froth recalls multiple forms of the interdependency of bee and human labour: bees gather pollen, some wild-growing and some perhaps human-cultivated, which combines with the enzymes in their saliva to activate the substance we know as honey; the honey, probably extracted from a hive (or skep, perhaps itself made of plant material) built by humans or bee-erected on a tree or other structure, becomes the golden, sticky substance by way of its production and storage in bee-forged combs. It is then harvested and 'clarified', which would have involved separating the liquid honey from the wax and residual pollen. And after mixing yet again, the resulting concoction is 'put in' the patient's 'greaved' eyes (morning and evening) 'with a fether' such that human and nonhuman animals and plants intra-act[21] to perform the cure.

In searching for such 'micro-practices' evident in early modern practice, however, we, unlike many ecofeminist theorists, turn to this more distant archive, where material practice is embodied by such recipes that unfold on the manuscript rather than print page. While Stacy Alaimo, for example, has her own repository of contemporary testimonials and imaginative fictions, those who work in early historical periods have much to excavate. As should be clear throughout this study, ecofeminists have a particular relationship to that historical archive. While that relationship can be seen to be in alignment with feminist excavation projects, the ecofeminist relationship to the early modern archive especially centres on the human-and-nonhuman exchange that might look different when exploring texts whose circulation and use was quite different from those sold on the streets of London. This focus means that those pieces that may otherwise have been considered by critics interested in 'the place(s) of women in Shakespeare's world', such as Phyllis Rackin, Natasha Korda and Wendy Wall, are otherwise interpreted and made meaningful.[22]

With this in mind, the appendix to this study highlights and provides an easily accessible catalogue of the resources (many of which have been heretofore noted) available to student and faculty researchers who may or may not have physical access to actual early modern material texts but who see the importance of putting Shakespeare's plays in dialogue with other early modern engagements with the environment. Numbering in the hundreds and scattered throughout archives in Britain and the US, these collections, as we have shown, uniquely reflect material practices as well as the animal, vegetable and mineral ingredients accessed by the early modern household. Various projects on both sides of the Atlantic are working to explore/preserve/interpret these practices and resources through digitization, digital humanities and experimental archaeological initiatives.

Living nature

As nature includes the air and earth itself, the metaphors of resuscitation or excavation ultimately fail us. Thus, ecofeminism is not only a theoretical frame, dependent on metaphor, but also a scholarly and lived *practice*. We see this lived practice in the activism of its proponents. Sylvia Bowerbank, as Mary O'Connor and Sara Mendelson have reminded us, was not only an important voice in early modern ecofeminist scholarship, but she also 'worked hard to bring to public attention the greening issues that were of vital importance to neighbours and local farmers'.[23] In *Earthcare*, Carolyn Merchant's sequel to *The Death of Nature*, she speaks of the relation between 'Women and the Progressive Conservation Crusade'.[24] And Noël Sturgeon begins her history of ecofeminist theory with a somewhat surreal account of a feminist protest.[25] In working with early modern history, we see the continuum of modern 'conservation crusades' and historical labour. Because the environment is shared among us all, ecofeminism acknowledges that it will take more than one individual, more than even a village, to halt carbon emissions and toxic run-off. As scholars, we recognize the importance of stepping out of our elite tenured positions, embracing the value of all work, and enlisting our students to be a part of the larger task. Through connecting our classrooms that are otherwise both geographically and temporally removed from each other to larger research goals and global crises, both teachers and students see a world outside of their immediate ambitions.

More importantly, the intellectual, pedagogical and practical work preserving recipes connects us to a time before rabid consumerism and the imminent destruction of our ecosystem. It was a time when every household grew a garden, most people walked to work and many made their own medicine. It was also a time when the plague sliced through city populations once a decade and chimney fires endangered neighbourhoods even more regularly. It may be a moment that seems so divorced from our present as to seem irrelevant, but our current rallying cries to conserve and dire forecasts of epidemic and drought make for startling proximity.

Thus ecofeminists (and others), while volunteering with local activist organizations, are inclined to plant comfrey, nourish earthworms, count birds and hive bees in an attempt to participate in the practices we study as well as to reconstitute a relationship with the environment that acknowledges our shared resilience and fragility. This investment in knowledge as practice puts us in alignment with projects such as Pamela Smith's explorations into 'craft knowledge and artisanal epistemology' through her 'making and knowing project'[26] and even the more light-hearted 'Cooking the Archive' series curated by Alyssa Connell and Marissa Nicosia.[27] What may previously have been cordoned off as a separate 'experimental archaeology', through these projects, is revealing itself as a truly interdisciplinary endeavour as scientists and historians encounter the book together. Making, growing and caretaking (and the recording of these processes) requires a different kind of close reading of texts, one that allows us to see textual moments – as well as lived existence – differently. Ecofeminists enter the archive looking for evidence of that existence and the intimacies and conflicts that evidence reveals. In the how-tos of each day, the diaries of household affairs and the records of the non-elite the early modern world becomes at once immediate and strange, profound and recognizable. In the continuities between text and experience, past and future, our current moment comes into high relief. Contrary to Carolyn Merchant's assertion, Nature never died, and the 'organic' was never really 'lost'. They were there all along; we just needed to start looking for/at them again.

APPENDIX: EXCAVATING NATURE

While two circumscribed and fee-based databases from Adam Matthew, Perdita and Defining Gender, have made some manuscripts available in digital format, libraries have been working to make their collections internationally accessible without cost. As of the publication of this book, at least three archives with substantial early modern recipe book collections have undertaken the task of digitizing their holdings. The Wellcome Library was the first of these, with over 130 of its more extensive pre-1800 collection now in digital format, and many of these have their individual recipes indexed and are thus searchable. In conducting these searches, one must be sure to check for exact spelling; that is, if looking for Syrup of Violets, one must creatively enter 'sirrup', 'sirup', 'surrup', 'surup', etc. along with the many variations of 'violet' (violet, vyolet, vilot) into the 'any text' window. Partial lists of the recipe as named by its main ingredient and not its ailment – otherwise found under 'For a cough' (coff, caughe) – will thus appear. While still limited, this search engine has been a valuable resource in the discovery of pest control recipes, for example, or the infamous 'Oil of Swallows', discussed by Michelle DiMeo and Rebecca Laroche in their essay on the subject.[1] For a full list, enter 'remedy books' in the 'Any text' window of the Manuscripts Archive search window. Two other collections are working to digitize their collections. The University of Pennsylvania Rare Book and Manuscript Library has made nineteen of its recipe manuscripts available through its Penn in Hand digitization project. To access a full list of these books, type in 'recipe books' in the Penn in Hand search box. This collection includes a relatively rare late sixteenth-century text, perhaps compiled in the very years that Shakespeare conceived of Rosalind.[2] While these digitized collections provide access to the manuscript images, however, they do not yet include transcriptions of them, which potentially limits the type of searchability they provide.

Through a grant from the Pine Tree Foundation, the Folger Shakespeare Library has been concertedly digitizing its receipt books into the LUNA digital image collection.[3] As the individual images are numerous, one should first narrow down to the particular manuscript or manuscripts one would like to see through the Folger catalogue[4] before turning to LUNA. From these digital images, these works are to be transcribed into the Early Modern Manuscripts Online (EMMO) project, an effort to create a searchable database of early modern manuscripts. As such, EMMO begins to address the problem of access to searchable *transcriptions* as it also builds on various local archival initiatives that seek to preserve the holdings of a particular institution. The Folger, however, also recognizes the importance of expanding beyond one archive and looks ultimately to make connections between various manuscript holdings across repositories. With a focus on crowdsourcing digitized manuscript recipe books and letters (for now), The Folger's partnership with Zooniverse in a new project, 'Shakespeare's World',[5] illustrates how the 'Citizen Science' model might be applied more broadly to Humanities work to make transcription a collective knowledge-making endeavour. And so we turn to how such partnerships have been featured in digital humanities projects thus far and how they might be imagined to do so even more in the future.

Researchers in the field may be well acquainted with databases centred on print texts such as Women Writers Online (WWO), Early English Books Online (EEBO), the Text Creation Partnership (TCP-EEBO) and the English Broadside Ballad Archive (EBBA), all of which provide unique windows into the question of early modern environments and have been invaluable in writing this monograph. At least in the first three of these, several print recipe collections such as Markham's *English Huswife* (1615), Hannah Woolley's *The Cook's Guide* (1664) and the Countess of Kent's *A Choice Manual* (1653) are searchable, but outside the Wellcome's and *defining gender*'s recipe titles index, the thousands of recipes held in manuscript collections are largely uncatalogued and unsearchable. Those scholars working extensively with these collections quickly start developing their own transcribed subcollections in an endeavour to be able to cross reference and come up with some (albeit limited) quantitative data.

With the cognizance of these individual projects, the Early Modern Recipes Online Collective (EMROC) was formed in September 2012, coordinating efforts across continents and time zones to 'link … hundreds of texts in repositories that may be thousands of miles apart, as well as creating a space for dialogue about the ideas and research generated around these texts'. The project's mission is fundamentally collaborative both in spirit and in practice, as it aims

> to include scholars, students and the general public in the preservation, transcription and analysis of recipes written in English from circa 1550–1800. The ultimate goal is an accessible and searchable corpus of recipe books currently in manuscript. By enabling users to search by ingredient, date, process, person, disease, and type, we will be able to learn a lot about how early modern people interacted with each other and with their environments.[6]

Encouraged by such endeavours as the Early Modern Letters Online (EMLO) project and its important offshoot Women's Early Modern Letters Online (WEMLO), EMROC seeks to cut across archives and bring books that otherwise could not be directly in contact within the same digital repository. As the Folger's is one of the largest collections of early modern receipt books, EMROC has begun by coordinating its efforts with the EMMO project. EMROC's steering committee includes medical, book, literary and food historians ... and, yes, ecofeminists. The collaborative approach of the group, its existence as a co-creative collective (drawing on the expertise of researchers, teachers and students alike) helps to realize some of the ecofeminist goals we have articulated here.

Webliography

Cooking the Archive, http://rarecooking.com
Defining Gender, http://www.gender.amdigital.co.uk
Early English Books Online, http://eebo.chadwyck.com/home
Early Modern Letters Online, http://emlo.bodleian.ox.ac.uk/
Early Modern Manuscripts Online, http://folgerpedia.folger.edu/Early_Modern_Manuscripts_Online_%28EMMO%29
Early Modern Recipes Online Collective, http://emroc.hypotheses.org/
English Broadside Ballad Archive, http://ebba.english.ucsb.edu
LUNA Digital Image Collection, http://folger.luna.edu
The Making and Knowing Project, http://www.makingandknowing.org
Penn in Hand, http://dla.library.upenn.edu/dla/medren/index.html
Perdita Project, http://www.amdigital.co.uk/m-collections/collection/perdita-manuscripts-1500-1700/
The Recipes Project, http://recipes.hypotheses.org/
Textual Creation Partnership, http://www.textcreationpartnership.org/tcp-eebo
Wellcome Archives and Manuscripts Catalogue, http://archives.wellcomelibrary.org
Women Writers Project, http://www.wwp.northeastern.edu/wwo/
Women's Early Modern Letters Online, http://blogs.plymouth.ac.uk/wemlo/resources/wemlo-catalogue/

NOTES

Preface

1 William Shakespeare, *As You Like It*, 2.3.66. All Shakespeare quotations are from *The Arden Shakespeare Complete Works*, third series, edited by Richard Proudfoot, Ann Thompson and David Scott Kastan (London and New York: Bloomsbury Arden, 2014 [1998]).

2 Donna Haraway, *When Species Meet* (Minneapolis: University of Minnesota Press, 2008), 31.

3 Astrida Neimanis, Cecilia Åsberg and Johan Hedrén, 'Four Problems, Four Directions for Environmental Humanities: Toward Critical Posthumanities for the Anthropocene'. *Ethics and the Environment* 20 (no. 1) (Spring 2015): 69.

4 Noël Sturgeon, *Ecofeminist Natures: Race, Gender, Feminist Theory, and Political Action* (New York and London: Routledge, 1997), 1.

5 See, for instance, Madeleine Somerville, 'Inequality of Environmentalism: Is Green Movement Exclusionary by Nature?' *Guardian*, 26 April 2016. http://www.theguardian.com/lifeandstyle/2016/apr/26/environmentalism-inequality-farmers-market-go-green (accessed 26 April 2016).

6 See Steve Mentz, 'After Sustainability'. *PMLA* 127 (no. 3) (May 2012): 586.

7 Ibid.

8 Neimanis, Åsberg and Hedrén, 'Four Problems, Four Directions', 69. The original quotation reads 'acknowledges' and 'nurtures'.

Introduction

1. Rob Nixon, *Slow Violence and the Environmentalism of the Poor* (Cambridge, MA and London: Harvard University Press, 2011), 2.
2. Noël Sturgeon, *Ecofeminist Natures: Race, Gender, Feminist Theory, and Political Action* (New York and London: Routledge, 1997), 168.
3. William Reuckert is attributed with the first published approach to the study of 'literature' and 'ecology'. See Cheryl Glotfelty and Harold Fromm, eds, *The Ecocriticism Reader: Landmarks in Literary Ecology* (Athens: University of Georgia Press, 1996). Here, Glotfelty famously defines ecocriticism as 'the study of the relationship between literature and the physical environment' (xviii).
4. Sturgeon, *Ecofeminist Natures*, 26.
5. Ibid., 27.
6. See especially Val Plumwood, *Feminism and the Mastery of Nature* (London: Routledge, 1993), *Environmental Culture: The Ecological Crisis of Reason* (Abingdon: Routledge, 2002) and 'Nature in the Active Voice'. *Australian Humanities Review* 46, May 2009. http://www.australianhumanitiesreview.org/archive/Issue-May-2009/plumwood.html (accessed 2 May 2016).
7. Victoria Davion, 'Is Ecofeminism Ecofeminist?' in *Ecological Feminism*, ed. Karen Warren (New York: Routledge, 1994), 8.
8. See Plumwood, *Environmental Culture*, where she writes that 'monological forms of rationality' are 'built on the model of the self as an isolated, atomistic self-contained individual, the separate self, [and] are not only unethical but also irrational and prudentially hazardous', whereas 'dialogical logics assist conflict resolution, conversation, and fair exchange' (33).
9. See Vandana Shiva, *Staying Alive: Women, Ecology, and Development* (Brooklyn and Boston: South End Press, 2010 [1988]).
10. Ibid., 6.

11 See Jason Moore, 'The Capitalocene, Part II: Abstract Social Nature and the Limits of Capital', 4. http://www.jasonwmoore.com/uploads/The_Capitalocene__Part_I__June_2014.pdf (accessed 2 May 2016).

12 Sturgeon, *Ecofeminist Natures*, 190, quoted from Karen Warren, 'Feminism and Ecology: Making Connections'. *Environmental Ethics* 9 (no. 1) (1987): 17 (emphasis in original).

13 Bruno Latour, *We Have Never Been Modern*, trans. Catherine Porter (Cambridge: Harvard University Press, 1993).

14 See, for example, Jane Bennett, *Vibrant Matter: A Political Ecology of Things* (Durham and London: Duke University Press, 2010).

15 Important exceptions to this are Mel Chen, *Animacies: Biopolitics, Racial Mattering, and Queer Affect* (Durham and London: Duke University Press, 2012) and Stacy Alaimo, *Bodily Natures: Science, Environment, and the Material Self* (Bloomington and Indianapolis: Indiana University Press, 2010).

16 Stacy Alaimo, *Undomesticated Ground: Recasting Nature as Feminine Space* (Ithaca: Cornell University Press, 2000), 18. See also Stacy Alaimo, 'Sustainable This, Sustainable That: The New Materialisms, Posthumanism, and Unknown Futures'. *PMLA* 127 (no. 3) (2012): 558–64.

17 See especially Val Plumwood, who in 'Nature in the Active Voice' argues for a recuperation of the agentic qualities of Nature (and women) as a way of simultaneously redressing both anthropocentrism *and* androcentrism.

18 Karen Barad, *Meeting the Universe Halfway: Quantum Physics and the Entanglement of Matter and Meaning* (Durham: Duke University Press, 2007), 59 (emphasis ours).

19 Moore, 'The Capitalocene, Part II', 2.

20 See, for instance, Chapter 1, 'Movements of Ecofeminism', in Sturgeon, *Ecofeminist Natures*, 23–58.

21 Alaimo, *Undomesticated Ground*, 10. See also Donna Haraway's notion of 'situated knowledges' in 'Situated Knowledges: The Science Question in Feminism and the

Privilege of Partial Perspective'. *Feminist Studies* 14 (no. 3) (Autumn 1988): 575–99.

22 Lynne Dickson Bruckner, 'N/nature and the Difference "She" Makes', in *Ecofeminist Approaches to Early Modernity*, eds Jennifer Munroe and Rebecca Laroche (New York: Palgrave Macmillan, 2011), 17.

23 Simon Estok, 'Afterword: Ecocriticism on the Lip of the Lion', in *Ecocritical Shakespeare*, eds Lynne Bruckner and Dan Brayton (Farnham: Ashgate, 2011), 243. From our introductory chapter, it should be clear that we do not agree with his assessment that ecocriticism has 'supplanted ecofeminism' (242).

24 Michelle DiMeo and Rebecca Laroche, 'On Elizabeth Isham's "Oil of Swallows": Animal Slaughter and Early Modern Women's Medical Recipes', in Munroe and Laroche, eds, *Ecofeminist Approaches to Early Modernity*, 87–104; Amy Tigner, 'Preserving Nature in Hannah Woolley's *The Queen-Like Closet; or Rich Cabinet*', in ibid., 129–52; and David Goldstein, 'Woolley's Mouse: Early Modern Recipe Books and the Uses of Nature' in ibid., 105–28.

25 Jennifer Munroe, 'First "Mother of Science": Milton's Eve, Knowledge, and Nature', in ibid., 37–55.

26 Rebecca Laroche, '"Cabbage and Roots" and the Difference of *Merry Wives*', in *The Merry Wives of Windsor: New Critical Essays*, eds Evelyn Gajowski and Phyllis Rackin (London and New York: Routledge, 2015), 184–94.

27 Rebecca Laroche and Jennifer Munroe, 'On a Bank of Rue; Or Materialist Ecofeminist Inquiry and the Garden of *Richard II*'. *Shakespeare Studies* 42 (2014): 42–50.

28 Jennifer Munroe, 'Is it Really Ecocritical If It Isn't Feminist?', in *Ecological Approaches to Early Modern Texts: A Field Guide to Reading and Teaching*, eds Jennifer Munroe, Edward J. Geisweidt and Lynne Dickson Bruckner (Aldershot and Burlington: Ashgate Press, 2015), 47. See also Rebecca Laroche, 'Ophelia's Plants and the Death of Violets', in *Ecocritical Shakespeare*, eds Bruckner and Brayton, 211–22; Jennifer Munroe, 'It's All About the Gillyvors: Engendering Art and Nature in *The Winter's Tale*' in ibid., 139–55; and

Jennifer Munroe, 'Shakespeare and Ecocriticism Reconsidered'. *Literature Compass* 12 (no. 9) (2015): 37–50.

29 Louise Noble, '"Bare and Desolate Now": Cultural Ecology and "The Description of Cookham"', in *Ecological Approaches to Early Modern Texts*, eds Munroe, Geisweidt and Bruckner, 99.

30 Hillary Nunn, 'On Vegetating Virgins: Greensickness and the Plant Realm in Early Modern Literature', in *The Indistinct Human in Renaissance Literature*, eds Jean Feerick and Vin Nardizzi (New York: Palgrave Macmillan, 2012), 170.

Chapter 1

1 Nunn, 'On Vegetating Virgins', 11.

2 For examples of how some have already begun to do this work, see especially the following: Goldstein, 'Woolley's Mouse' and DiMeo and Laroche, 'On Elizabeth Isham's "Oil of Swallows"', 87–104.

3 Wendy Wall, *Staging Domesticity: Household Work and English Identity in Early Modern Drama* (Cambridge: Cambridge University Press, 2002).

4 Natasha Korda, *Shakespeare's Domestic Economies: Gender and Property in Early Modern England* (Philadelphia: University of Pennsylvania Press, 2002), 3.

5 See Alaimo, *Bodily Natures* for a more elaborated discussion of 'transcorporeality'.

6 Scholars have focused on the concept of 'oikos', a concept in which household economy and household ecology intersect, but this focus has not tended to parse out the gendered qualities of both.

7 For further discussion about this concept, see Plumwood, 'Nature in the Active Voice'.

8 See Korda, *Shakespeare's Domestic Economies*.

9 Wall, *Staging Domesticity*, 2.

10 Ibid., 2–3.

11 For further discussion of the terms 'intraconnection' and 'entanglements', see Barad, *Meeting the Universe Halfway* and 'Posthumanist Performativity: Toward an Understanding of How Matter Comes to Matter'. *Signs: Journal of Women in Culture and Society* 28 (no. 3) (2003): 801–31.

12 Jane Bennett, *Vibrant Matter: A Political Ecology of Things* (Durham and London: Duke University Press, 2010), 4.

13 See Sir Francis Bacon *The New Organon Or: True Directions Concerning the Interpretation of Nature*, Book 1, Aphorism 1, 4. http://www.earlymoderntexts.com/assets/pdfs/bacon1620.pdf (accessed 2 May 2016).

14 Bennett, *Vibrant Matter*, 13–14.

15 Plumwood, *Environmental Culture*, 29.

16 See Feerick and Nardizzi, eds, *The Indistinct Human in Renaissance Literature* (New York: Palgrave Macmillan, 2012).

17 Plumwood, *Environmental Culture*, 45–6.

18 Donna Haraway, 'Anthropocene, Capitalocene, Chthulucene: Staying with the Trouble' (9 May 2014). https://vimeo.com/97663518 (accessed 2 May 2016).

19 See Loraine Daston and Katharine Park, eds, *Wonders and the Order of Nature* (New York: Zone, 1998) and Mary Floyd-Wilson, *Occult Knowledge: Science and Gender on the Shakespearean Stage* (Cambridge: Cambridge University Press, 2013).

20 In this way, Haraway's 'Chthulucene' serves as a term that conveys the reprioritization of 'wonder' inherent to the term 'preternatural', but specifically invokes at the same time an alternative approach to how we got ourselves into the environmental pickle we now find ourselves (most of us anyway) trying to get out of. See Haraway, 'Anthropocene, Capitalocene, Chthulucene'.

21 Mary Floyd-Wilson and Garrett Sullivan, eds, *Environment and Embodiment in Early Modern England* (Basingstoke and New York: Palgrave Macmillan, 2007), 3.

22 Ibid.

23 See Bennett, *Vibrant Matter*.

24 See Alaimo, *Bodily Natures*.

25 Harry Heft, 'Affordances, Dynamic Experience, and the Challenge of Reification'. *Ecological Psychology* 15 (no. 2): 164. http://www.faculty.virginia.edu/perlab/misc/ReadingMeeting/Heft,2003.pdf (accessed 2 May 2016). See also Julia Reinhard Lupton, 'The Renaissance Res Publica of Furniture', in *Animal, Vegetable, Mineral: Ethics and Objects*, ed. Jeffrey Jerome Cohen (Washington: Oliphaunt, 2012), 211–36.

26 Bennett, *Vibrant Matter*, 4.

27 Ian Bogost, *Alien Phenomenology; Or What It's Like to Be a Thing* (Minneapolis and London: University of Minnesota Press, 2012), 74.

28 See Heft, 'Affordances, Dynamic Experience, and the Challenge of Reification', 155. We are grateful for Julia Reinhardt Lupton's 'The Renaissance Res Publica of Furniture', 211–36, which brought Heft's work to our attention.

29 Heft, 'Affordances', 155.

30 See Lupton, 'The Renaissance Res Publica', where she brings these things together in her piece on household furniture, notably the 'stool'.

31 Michael Pollan's chapter on intoxication and marijuana in *The Botany of Desire* looks aslant at this aspect (New York: Random House, 2001), 111–80.

32 Rebecca Laroche, 'Ophelia's Plants and the Death of Violets', in *Ecocritical Shakespeare*, eds Bruckner and Brayton, 211–22.

33 Korda, *Shakespeare's Domestic Economies*, 1.

34 Lady Frances Catchmay, 'A Booke of Medicens', Wellcome MS 184a, f.14v. Transcription credit goes to Breanne Weber, MA Student at UNC Charlotte.

35 We are reminded of David Goldstein's analysis of Hannah Woolley's mouse. Goldstein, 'Woolley's Mouse', 105–28.

36 Oliver Millman, 'Climate change may have helped spread Zika virus, according to WHO scientists', *Guardian*, 11 February 2016. http://www.theguardian.com/world/2016/feb/11/climate-change-zika-virus-south-central-america-mosquitos (accessed 2 May 2016).

37 Ibid.
38 Archie Bland, 'Should we wipe mosquitos off the face of the Earth'. *Guardian*, 10 February 2016. http://www.theguardian.com/global/2016/feb/10/should-we-wipe-mosquitoes-off-the-face-of-the-earth (accessed 2 May 2016).
39 Ibid.
40 Ibid.

Chapter 2

1 William Shakespeare, *A Midsummer Night's Dream*, 5.1.162.
2 Gervase Markham, *The Second Book of The English Husbandman* (London, 1614), 43. Transcription Text Creation Partnership.
3 Plumwood, 'Nature in the Active Voice'.
4 Plumwood, *Environmental Culture*, 51, quoted in *Ecological Approaches to Early Modern Texts*, eds Munroe, Geisweidt and Bruckner, 3.
5 Alaimo, *Bodily Natures*, 2.
6 Jeanne Addison Roberts, *The Shakespearean Wild* (Lincoln: University of Nebraska Press, 1994), 2.
7 Ibid.
8 Those exceptions include Karen Raber, *Animal Bodies, Renaissance Culture* (Philadelphia: University of Pennsylvania Press, 2013) and Laurie Shannon, *The Accommodated Animal: Cosmopolity in Shakespearean Locales* (Chicago: University of Chicago Press, 2013), both of which consider gender categories at various points.
9 See, for example, Lowell Duckert, 'Exit, Pursued by a Polar Bear (More to Follow)'. *Upstart*, 4 June 2013). http://www.clemson.edu/upstart/Essays/exit-pursued-by-a-polar-bear/exit-pursued-by-a-polar-bear.xhtml (accessed 30 November 2015) and Andreas Höefele, *Stage Stake, and Scaffold: Humans and Animals in Shakespeare's Theatre* (Oxford: Oxford University Press, 2011). See also Gabriel Egan's chapter on

this subject, 'Animals in Shakespearean Ecocriticism', in *Shakespeare and Ecocritical Theory* (London: Bloomsbury/Arden, 2015), 95–119.

10 Höefele, *Stage, Stake, and Scaffold*.

11 Simon Estok, *Ecocriticism and Shakespeare: Reading Ecophobia* (New York: Palgrave, 2011).

12 Thomas Moffat, *Theatre of Insects, or the Lesser Living Creatures*, printed with Edward Topsel, *The History of Four-Footed Beasts and Serpents* (London, 1658); Todd Borlik, in 'Fairy-Lore as Folk Entomology in Shakespeare's England', in *Performing Animals*, Karen Raber, ed. (yet unpublished monograph, Penn State University Press); Keith Botelho, *Little Beasts: Cultures of the Hive in Renaissance England*, forthcoming; Joseph Campana, 'The Bee and the Sovereign: Political Entomology and the Problem of Scale'. *Shakespeare Studies* 41 (2013): 94–113; and Karen Raber, 'Vermin and Parasites: Shakespeare's Animal Architectures', in *Ecocritical Shakespeare*, Bruckner and Brayton, eds, 13–32.

13 Of course, many have commented on this fly, but our attention is to the fly as fly, not as symbol or harbinger of death, not as synecdoche of the lower rungs of the chain of being.

14 Gervase Markham, *The Second Booke of The English Husbandman* (London, 1614), 43. Transcription from the Text Creation Partnership, http://quod.lib.umich.edu/e/eebogroup/ (accessed 5 May 2016).

15 See, for instance, Timothy Morton, 'Everything We Need: Scarcity, Scale, Hyper-Objects'. *Architectural Design* 82 (no. 4) (2012): 79.

16 Markham, *The Second Booke of the English Husbandman*, 46.

17 Ibid., 48.

18 See *Country Contentments, or The English Huswife* (London, for Roger Jackson, 1623): 3 (STC 17395.7).

19 Wendy Wall, *Recipes for Thought: Knowledge and Taste in the Early Modern English Kitchen* (Philadelphia: University of Pennsylvania Press, 2016), 44.

20 Elizabeth Jacob et al., 'Physicall and Chyrurgicall Receipts', Wellcome MS 3009, Digital Image 0058.
21 'Johnson Family recipe book', Wellcome MS 3082, Digital Image 7.
22 Anonymous, 'Cookery books: 17th/18th century', Wellcome MS 1795, Digital Image 66; Anne Brumwich, 'Her Book of Receipts or Medicines', Wellcome MS 160, Digital Image 0110.
23 See the respective Prefaces to Markham, *The Second Booke of the English Husbandman* and *Countrey Contentments*.
24 Goldstein, 'Woolley's Mouse', 105–28.
25 Ibid., 112.
26 Hannah Woolley, *Supplement to the Queen-Like Closet* (London, 1674), 23.
27 See Natasha Korda, who situates this scene and the 'household cates' as household objects, the consumable goods associated with women in the period. See especially *Shakespeare's Domestic Economies*, 52–75.
28 Royal Shakespeare Company, *The Taming of the Shrew: Live from Shakespeare's Globe* (New York: Films Media Group, c. 2012 [2013]), time register 1:01:58.
29 *Oxford English Dictionary* [online] (accessed 25 November 2015). Subsequent references included in the text.
30 The development as a term for 'itinerant worker' in the United States fails the imagination, but the *OED* insists on placing these uses together as they are both terms of contempt.
31 All references are taken from the Early English Ballad Archive. http://ebba.english.ucsb.edu/ (accessed 5 September 2015).
32 Alaimo, *Bodily Natures*, 2.
33 Lady Frances Catchmay, 'A Booke of Medicens', Wellcome MS 184a, digital image 10. http://archives.wellcome.ac.uk/recipebooks/MS184A/MS184A_0010.pdf (accessed 25 November 2015).
34 Anne Brumwich et al., Wellcome MS 160, digital image 36. http://archives.wellcome.ac.uk/recipebooks/MS160/MS160_0036.pdf (accessed 25 November 2015). See Jennifer Sherman Roberts 'Wigging Out: Mrs. Corlyon's Method for

Extracting Earwigs from the Ear' and the discussion of the early modern fear of earwigs entering the ear and consequently the brain at http://recipes.hypotheses.org/5634 (accessed 1 November 2015).

35 Alaimo, *Bodily Natures*, 2. With this theory, we also return to the 'in here' of Goldstein's analysis above.

36 Ibid., 11.

37 Randall Martin, '"I Wish You the Joy of the Worm"': Evolutionary Ecology in *Hamlet* and *Antony and Cleopatra*', in *Shakespeare and Ecology* (Oxford: Oxford University Press, 2015), 134–65.

38 Markham, *The Second Booke of the English Husbandman*, 46–7.

39 Boyle Family, 'Recipe Book', Wellcome MS 1340, digital image 89. http://archives.wellcome.ac.uk/recipebooks/MS1340/MS1340_0089.pdf (accessed 1 November 2015).

40 Coco Ballantyne, 'Strange But True: Antibacterial Products May Do More Harm Than Good'. *Scientific American*, 7 June 2007. http://www.scientificamerican.com/article/strange-but-true-antibacterial-products-may-do-more-harm-than-good/ (accessed 3 May 2016).

41 Michael Pollan, 'Some of My Best Friends Are Germs'. *New York Times Magazine*, 15 May 2013. http://www.nytimes.com/2013/05/19/magazine/say-hello-to-the-100-trillion-bacteria-that-make-up-your-microbiome.html?pagewanted=all&_r=0 (accessed 3 May 2016).

42 Liz Gross, 'Pollution, Poverty, and People of Color: Don't Drink the Water'. *Scientific American*, 12 June 2012. http://www.scientificamerican.com/article/pollution-poverty-people-color-dont-drink-water/ (accessed 5 May 2016).

43 Thanks to Michelle Perez, whose work in Shakespeare and Ecofeminist Theory in spring 2015 (at UC Colorado Springs) inspired many of the insights here.

44 Sara Pennell, 'Pots and Pans History: The Material Culture of the Kitchen in Early Modern England'. *Journal of Design History* 11 (no. 3) (1998): 201–16.

45 Anonymous, *A Closet for Ladies and Gentlevvomen* (London,

1608). Transcription from the Text Creation Partnership, http://quod.lib.umich.edu/e/eebogroup/ (accessed 5 May 2016).

46 A.T., *A rich store-house or treasury for the diseased* (London 1596), n.p. (emphasis ours). Transcription from the Text Creation Partnership, http://quod.lib.umich.edu/e/eebogroup/ (accessed 5 May 2016).

47 D. S. Grey, ed., *Samuel Pepys' Diary*. http://www.pepys.info/fire.html (accessed 20 November 2015).

48 John Evelyn, journal entry, 3 September 1666, reproduced in ibid.

49 Ibid. See also Suzanne Phillips, *Hidden Killers of the Tudor Home*, BBC, 2015 (film).

50 Grey, *Samuel Pepys' Diary*, 8 January 1660.

51 Anne Trapnel, *The Cry of a Stone* (London 1654). Women Writers Online. http://www.wwp.northeastern.edu/wwo (accessed 15 August 2015), G1v.

52 See Wall on distillation in *Recipes for Thought*, 183–9.

53 Wall, *Staging Domesticity*.

54 John Ingold, 'Decade After Hayman Fire, Questions Linger about Fire's Start'. *Denver Post*, 3 June 2012. http://www.denverpost.com/ci_20769983/decade-after-hayman-fire-questions-linger-about-fires (accessed 3 May 2016).

55 Alaimo, *Bodily Natures*, 14.

56 Ibid., 17.

Chapter 3

1 All Shakespeare quotations are from *The Arden Shakespeare Complete Works*, eds Proudfoot, Thompson and Kastan. *KL* 1.1.87–9.

2 Bacon, *The New Organon*. http://www.earlymoderntexts.com/assets/pdfs/bacon1620.pdf (accessed 2 May 2016).

3 Plumwood, *Environmental Culture*, 97.

4 Haraway, 'Anthropocene, Capitalocene, Chthulucene'.

5 Alaimo, *Bodily Natures*, 2. See also our discussion of this concept in the Introduction, Chapter 1 and Chapter 2.

6   Steven Mentz, 'Strange Weather in King Lear'. *Shakespeare* 6 (2010): 139. http://stevementz.com/wp-content/uploads/2012/07/Strange-Weather-in-King-Lear.pdf (accessed 4 May 2016).

7   See Laurie Shannon, *The Accommodated Animal: Cosmopolity in Shakespearean Locales* (Chicago: University of Chicago Press, 2013).

8   See Todd Borlik, *Ecocriticism and Early Modern Literature: Green Pastures* (New York: Routledge, 2011), 129.

9   This wonder is perhaps reminiscent of what Haraway recently identified as the epoch she believes we have entered/are entering today, as the arts/humanities/sciences recognize the multiplicity and uncertainty – the 'so far' and not yet known – that she believes will help us address environmental crises more effectively than the 'Anthropocene' does; perhaps Shakespeare's plays come from a similar place, and understanding how they theorize the subject–object relations may help us too – where past and present come together.

10 Here we intentionally deviate from such scholars as Jane Bennett and Bruno Latour, whose ideas still depend on a notion of the Anthropocene. Instead, by drawing attention to the way the play reorients human–nonhuman relations to include a specific focus on gendered and class identity, we evoke a different term for our epoch: The Capitalocene. See Moore, 'The Capitalocene, Part II', 4.

11 This moment in Lear calls to mind a recent piece from *The Guardian*, which details an assault on the homeless by which (in London, Hamburg, New York and elsewhere) city officials install various structural elements to prevent men and women from sleeping in public spaces. Shakespeare, it would seem, has much to teach them. See Alex Andreou, 'Anti-Homeless Spikes: "Sleeping Rough Opened My Eyes to the City's Barbed Cruelty"'. *Guardian*, 18 February 2015. http://www.theguardian.com/society/2015/feb/18/defensive-architecture-keeps-poverty-unseen-and-makes-us-more-hostile (accessed 4 May 2016). And see a follow-up story, where artists turned the spikes into an act of artful defiance. Robbie Couch, 'Artists Got Fed Up With These "Anti-Homeless Spikes." So They Made Them a Bit More …Comfy'. *Upworthy*, 24 July 2015.

http://www.upworthy.com/artists-got-fed-up-with-these-anti-homeless-spikes-so-they-made-them-a-bit-more-comfy?c=ufb1 (accessed 4 May 2016).

12 Mentz, 'Strange Weather', 143.

13 Alaimo, *Bodily Natures*.

14 For a more detailed reading of the agricultural references in *Lear*, see Jayne Archer et al., 'The Autumn King: Remembering the Land in *King Lear*'. *Shakespeare Quarterly* 63 (no. 4) (Winter 2012): 518–43.

15 In thinking about the implications of this passage further, we may turn to Jessica Rosenberg's stirring reading of rhetorical and botanical 'vertue' in 'Poetic Language, Practical Handbooks, and the "Vertues" of Plants', in *Ecological Approaches to Early Modern English Texts*, eds Munroe, Geisweidt and Bruckner (Farnham: Ashgate, 2015), 61–70.

16 Folger MS v.a.388, 1.

17 Haraway, 'Situated Knowledges', 592.

18 Ibid., 598. Cf. Wendy Wall's brief discussion of 'situated knowledge' differently with reference to the work of Sara Pennell and Elizabeth Spiller: *Recipes for Thought* (Philadelphia: University of Pennsylvania Press, 2015), 211.

19 Carol Neely calls Lear's madness a move from supernatural to natural, but by this Neely means more the broader shift from attributing events to the gods, for instance, to using logic and reason – what we can see, touch, and hear, to explain events. Such a focus on this shift both emphasizes human perception of the nonhuman world and suggests a relation to it that is more distinct – more of an either/or – than we propose here. *Distracted Subjects: Madness and Gender in Shakespeare and Early Modern Culture* (Ithaca: Cornell University Press, 2004), 46–68.

20 Simon Estok, who insists that we think of the storm as an actual meteorological event, is a notable exception to this. However, Estok argues that the result of Lear's encounter with the storm reinforces a relation to the nonhuman world that Estok calls 'ecophobia'. See *Ecocriticism and Shakespeare: Reading Ecophobia* (New York: Palgrave, 2011).

21 Mentz, 'Strange Weather'.

22 Plumwood, *Environmental Culture*, 45–6.

23 Floyd-Wilson, *Occult Knowledge*, 28–46.

24 This name, Gerard de Narbon, evokes the well-known herbalist John Gerard, and so the murkiness about the potency of the cure (whether Helena's or her father's) extrapolates more broadly onto the question of whether medical remedies take their power from their amateur (and largely female) practitioners or the (male) professionals.

25 Such cures were often the domain of laywomen; at the same time, the *fistula-in-ano* was notoriously difficult to cure, so much so that 'many surgeons refused to treat them'. See Catherine Field, '"Sweet Practicer, Thy Physic I Will Try": Helena and Her "Good Receipt" in *All's Well That Ends Well*', in *All's Well That Ends Well: Critical Essays*, ed. Gary Waller (New York and London: Routledge, 2007), 195. See also, Wendy Wall's discussion of how '*All's Well* capitalizes on the paradoxes and problems of preservation circulating in popular printed recipes in the book market in England'. *Recipes for Thought*, 183.

26 Ibid.

27 Catchmay, 'A Booke of Medicens' Wellcome MS 184a, fols. 38v–39r (digital image 39). For other examples of fistula recipes see Field, '"Sweet Practicer"' and Wall, *Recipes for Thought*, 178.

28 Bruce Boehrer, 'The Privy and Its Double: Scatology and Satire in Shakespeare's Theater', in *The Blackwell Companion to Shakespeare: The Poems, Problem Comedies, and Late Plays*, eds Jean Howard and Richard Dutton (Oxford: Blackwell Press, 2003). See Boehrer's claim that the king's 'disease is introduced in the context of the sufferer's resignation', but this resignation is precisely what moves the king to allow Helena to cure him, so it is a good thing (83).

29 In drafting this chapter, we have found ourselves eerily forecasting the subject of Julian Yates' presentation 'Macbeth's Bubbles', Shakespeare Association of America, New Orleans, 26 March 2016, where he too 'reorients' around the weird sisters, but to different theoretical ends.

30 Plumwood, *Environmental Culture*, 33.
31 Ibid., 9, 19.
32 As Wall notes, the list includes 'limbs of foreigners, heretics, and murder victims' (*Staging Domesticity*, 199).
33 Ibid. Women's domestic medicine recipes also used ingredients like those used by the sisters, including, for instance, 'handfulles of Dragon or Serpentes toungue', found in a recipe from the Mrs Corlyon book. Corlyon, fol. 159; it is not certain whether serpent's (or adder's) tongue was plant or animal, as English adder's tongue is a native British fern, and so the reference is not necessarily to the serpent with demonic associations.
34 Loraine Daston, 'The Nature of Nature in Early Modern Europe'. *Configurations* 6 (1998): 4. http://isites.harvard.edu/fs/docs/icb.topic1360696.files/Daston-Nature%20of%20Nature%20abr.pdf (accessed 5 June 2015).
35 David Wescott, 'Survival of the Fittest in the English Department'. *The Chronicle of Higher Education*, 1 May 2015. http://chronicle.com/article/Jonathan-Gottschalls-Fighting/229763/ (accessed 4 May 2016).

Chapter 4

1 William Shakespeare, *As You Like It*, 5.3.29. All Shakespeare quotations are from *The Arden Shakespeare Complete Works*, eds Proudfoot, Thompson and Kastan.
2 Anne Layfielde, 'Recipe Book of Anne Layfielde', College of Physicians of Philadelphia, MS 10a214, 34.
3 Barbara Johnson, *Persons and Things* (Cambridge: Harvard University Press, 2008), 17.
4 Ian Bogost, *Alien Phenomenology; or What It's Like to Be a Thing* (Minneapolis and London: University of Minnesota Press, 2012).
5 Johnson, *Persons and Things*, 17.
6 Leonard Barkan, '"Living Sculptures": Ovid, Michelangelo,

and *The Winter's Tale*'. *ELH*, 48.4 (1981): 639–67; and Barbara Roche Rico, 'From "Speechless Dialect" to "Prosperous Art": Shakespeare's Recasting of the Pygmalion Image'. *Huntington Library Quarterly: A Journal for the History and Interpretation of English and American Civilization* 48 (no. 3) (1985): 285–95. See also Sarah Annes Brown, 'Queering Pygmalion: Ovid, Euripides and *The Winter's Tale*', in *Shakespeare's Erotic Mythology and Ovidian Renaissance Culture*, ed. Agnès Lafont (Farnham: Ashgate, 2013), 139–52; and A. D. Nuttall, '*The Winter's Tale*: Ovid Transformed', in *Shakespeare's Ovid: The Metamorphoses in the Plays and Poems*, ed. A. B. Taylor (Cambridge: Cambridge University Press, 2000), 138–9.

7   Jennifer Waldron, 'Of Stones and Stony Hearts: Desdemona, Hermione, and Post-Reformation Theater', in *The Indistinct Human in Renaissance Literature*, eds Feerick and Nardizzi, 205–27.

8   Patricia Southard Gourlay, '"O My Most Sacred Lady": Female Metaphor in *The Winter's Tale*', in *The Winter's Tale: Critical Essays*, ed. Maurice Hunt (New York: Garland, 1995), 273. See also Abbe Blum, '"Strike All That Look Upon With Mar[b]le": Monumentalizing Women in Shakespeare's Plays', in *The Englishwoman in Print: Counterbalancing the Canon*, eds Anne M. Haselkorn and Betty S. Travitsky (Amherst: University of Massachusetts Press, 1990), 99–118; and Katherine R. Kellet, 'Petrarchan Desire, the Female Ghost, and *The Winter's Tale*', in *Staging the Blazon in Early Modern English Theater*, eds Deborah Uman and Sara Morrison (Farnham: Ashgate, 2013), 25–36. All of these readings are then interrupted by the character's ageing, dubbed 'the carver's excellence' (5.3) by Paulina.

9   See our Introduction and Chapter 1, where we discuss this term more at length.

10 See Chapter 1, where we discuss more at length the work of Harry Heft and the contribution we believe his concept of 'affordances' makes to ecofeminist work.

11 See Timothy Morton, 'Treating Objects Like Women: Feminist Ontology and the Question of Essence', in *International Perspectives in Feminist Ecocriticism*, eds Greta Gaard,

Serpil Opperman and Simon Estok (New York and London: Routledge, 2013), 56–69.

12 Nancy Vickers, 'Diana Described: Scattered Women, Scattered Rhymes', in *Writing and Sexual Difference*, ed. Elizabeth Abel (Chicago: University of Chicago Press, 1982), 95–109.

13 Ibid., 96.

14 Ibid., 109. Interestingly, if we return to the implications of our Hermione allegory, this kind of feminist critique resorts to a vocabulary that is later similarly used by OOO and other posthumanist theorizations with regard to objects themselves. As John Freccero writes about Laura, 'Like the Poetry that celebrates her, she gains immortality at the price of vitality and historicity': John Freccero, 'The Fig Tree and the Laurel: Petrarch's Poetics'. *Diacritics* 4 (Spring 1975): 38–9, quoted in Vickers, 'Diana Described', 102. Again, for feminist theorists, returning vitality to a being to which it had been denied is nothing new, but in looking back to early feminism, the valuing of 'historicity' is one that must be brought forward into discussions of objects.

15 See David Schalkwyk, *Speech and Performance in Shakespeare's Sonnets and Plays* (Cambridge: Cambridge University Press, 2002).

16 Jeffrey Cohen, *Stone: An Ecology of the Inhuman* (Minneapolis: University of Minneapolis Press, 2015).

17 As Leah Knight remarks while limiting the concept of motion to that of the early moderns, 'a moving tree is much less farfetched than a moving rock'. *Reading Green in Early Modern England* (Farnham and Burlington: Ashgate, 2014), 66. She writes, 'The wonder of a moving tree is, of course, considerably more impressive than the ordinary activities of any footed or finned thing; at the same time, since branches naturally bend in the breeze and petals and leaves unfurl, flutter, and fall. It is precisely this intermediate quality about the mobility of vegetation, a quality seeming to place plant on a middle ground between agency and objecthood, that may have made greenery a particularly attractive locus for fantasies about enhancing some earthly inhabitants with an additional degree of liveliness' (66).

18 See *Edmund Spenser's Poetry: A Norton Critical Edition*, 4th edn, eds Anne Lake Prescott and Andrew D. Hadfield (New York: W. W. Norton & Co., 2014).

19 Wall, *Recipes for Thought*; Hillary Nunn, 'Elizabeth Downing's Busy Month of May'. *The Recipes Project*, http://recipes.hypotheses.org/3776 (accessed 7 September 2016).

20 Sarah Longe, 'A Booke of Receiptes', Folger MS v.a.425, fol.19v.

21 'grace' n. 4a, *Oxford English Dictionary* (online).

22 'grace' n. 14b, *OED* (online).

23 'grace,' n. 13b, *OED* (online).

24 Hugh Plat, *Floraes Paradise* (London 1608), 90–2, emphasis ours.

25 For discussions of seasonal time in Shakespeare's *Sonnets*, see Dympna Callaghan, 'Confounded By Winter: Speeding Time in Shakespeare's Sonnets', in *A Companion to Shakespeare's Sonnets*, ed. Michael Schoenfeldt (Chichester: Wiley-Blackwell, 2010), 104–18; Rebecca Laroche, 'Roses in Winter: Recipe Ecologies and Shakespeare's Sonnets', in *Ecological Approaches to Early Modern English Texts*, eds Munroe, Geisweidt and Bruckner; Jessica Rosenberg, 'The Point of the Couplet: Shakespeare's Sonnets and Tusser's *A Hundreth Good Points of Husbandrie*'. *ELH* 83 (no. 1) (Spring 2016): 1–41.

26 Plat, *Floraes Paradise*, 104.

27 Heft, 'Affordances', 161.

28 Laroche articulates this understanding in 'Roses in Winter', cited above.

29 Jennifer Munroe, Amy Tigner and others have worked extensively to uncover the actual gardens that surround these fictional ones. Jennifer Munroe, *Gender and the Garden in Early Modern English Literature* (Burlington: Ashgate, 2008); Amy Tigner, *Literature and the Renaissance Garden from Elizabeth I to Charles II* (Burlington: Ashgate, 2012).

30 Bryn Mawr MS 19, fol. 40. Maria Thynne, 'Letters', in *Lay by your Needles Ladies, Take the Pen: Writing Women in England, 1500–1700*, eds Suzanne Trill, Kate Chedgzoy and Melanie Osborne (London: St Martin's Press, 1997),

76–7; Rebecca Laroche and Jennifer Munroe, 'On a Bank of Rue: Or Material Ecofeminist Inquiry and the Garden of *Richard II*'. *Shakespeare Studies* 42: 42–50. See also Laroche, 'Ophelia's Plants and the Death of Violets', in *Ecocritical Shakespeare*, eds Bruckner and Brayton (Burlington: Ashgate, 2011), 211–22.

31   Natasha Korda, *Labors Lost: Women's Work and the Early Modern English Stage* (Philadelphia: University of Pennsylvania Press, 2011), 31.

32   Patrick G. Hogan, Jr, 'Marvell's "Vegetable Love"'. *Studies in Philology* 60 (no. 1) (January 1963): 1–11. For an interrogation of the relationship between OOO's approach and the theories of the soul articulated by Aristotle, see Kellie Robertson, 'Abusing Aristotle', in *Speculative Medievalisms: Discography*, eds Eileen A. Joy, Anna Klosowska, Nicola Masciandro and Michael O'Rourke (New York: Punctum, 2013), 159–72. https://www.academia.edu/10235881/Abusing_ Aristotle (accessed 5 May 2016).

33   Nunn, 'On Vegetating Virgins', 159–177.

34   Jean Howard, 'Female Agency in *All's Well That Ends Well*'. *AUMLA: Journal of the Australasian Universities Modern Language and Literature Association* 106 (November 2006): 43–60.

35   Erin Ellerbeck, 'Adoption and the Language of Horticulture in *All's Well That Ends Well*'. *SEL* 51 (no. 2) (2011): 306, 2.

36   Phyllis Rackin, *Shakespeare and Women* (Oxford: Oxford University Press, 2005), 82. See also, for instance, Laura L. Levine, *Men in Women's Clothing: Anti-Theatricality and Effeminization, 1579–1642* (Cambridge: Cambridge University Press, 1994); Valerie, M. Traub, Lindsay Kaplan and Dympna Callaghan, eds, *Feminist Readings of Early Modern Culture: Emerging Subjects* (Cambridge: Cambridge University Press, 1996); and Dympna Callaghan, *Shakespeare Without Women: Representing Gender and Race on the Renaissance Stage* (New York: Routledge, 2000).

37   Rackin, *Shakespeare and Women*, 75.

38   Plumwood, 'Nature in the Active Voice'.

39 For a parallel ecofeminist reading see Munroe, '"It's all about the gillvors": Art and Nature in The Winter's Tale', 139–55.

40 'take', III.13b, *Oxford English Dictionary* [online]. Subsequent references to meanings of 'take' included in the text as part of the analysis.

41 This insight dialogues beautifully with Wall's insight that 'as home herbalists, gardeners, and pharmacists, early modern women were instructed to submit to time by fully understanding and inhabiting the rhythms of change over the year'. *Recipes for Thought*, 171.

42 Thanks to Paula Pyne for articulating this so well in class discussion, ENGL 4970, Shakespeare and Ecofeminist Theory, University of Colorado Springs, Colorado, Spring Term 2015.

43 See, for instance, J. Lamont, 'Trait Body Shame Predicts Health Outcomes in College Women: A Longitudinal Investigation'. *Journal of Behavioral Medicine* 38 (no. 6) (December 2015): 998–1008. doi: 10.1007/s10865-015-9659-9, ePub 2015 July 23, http://www.ncbi.nlm.nih.gov/pubmed/26201456 (accessed 5 May 2016). Also Rebecca Adams, 'Body Shame May Actually Be Making Women Sick, Study Suggests'. *Huffington Post*, 4 August 2015. http://www.huffingtonpost.com/entry/body-shame-may-be-making-women-sick_us_55c0c54be4b06363d5a363db? (accessed 5 May 2016).

44 Roberto A. Ferdman, 'France is Making It Illegal for Supermarkets to Throw Away Edible Food'. *Washington Post*, 22 May 2015. https://www.washingtonpost.com/news/wonk/wp/2015/05/22/france-is-making-it-illegal-for-supermarkets-to-throw-away-edible-food/ (accessed 5 May 2016).

45 Karolyn Coorsh, 'Would You Buy Ugly Vegetables? That's How a Grocery Chain Fights Waste'. 29 July 2014. http://www.ctvnews.ca/world/would-you-buy-ugly-vegetables-that-s-how-a-grocery-chain-fights-waste-1.1938024 (accessed 5 May 2016).

46 Curt Nikisch, 'Trader Joe's Ex-President Opens Store with Aging Food and Cheap Meals'. 4 June 2015. http://www.npr.org/sections/thesalt/2015/06/04/411777947/

trader-joes-ex-president-opens-store-with-aging-food-and-cheap-meals (accessed 5 May 2016).

47   Imperfect Produce (online delivery company). http://www.imperfectproduce.com/home/ (accessed 5 May 2016).

48   Ferdman, 'France is Making It Illegal'.

49   See Allison Aubrey, 'From Ugly to Hip: Misfit Fruits and Veggies Coming to Whole Foods'. 7 March 2016. http://www.npr.org/sections/thesalt/2016/03/07/469530045/from-ugly-to-hip-misfit-fruits-and-veggies-coming-to-whole-foods (accessed 5 May 2016).

50   Further consideration may be applied to the fact that two of his lower-status male characters, Quince and LaVatch (vetch), also bear botanical names.

Conclusion

1   *WT* 5.3.100–4.

2   Margaret Baker, 'Receipt Book of Margaret Baker', Folger MS 619, fol. 24r.

3   Carolyn Merchant, *The Death of Nature: Women, Ecology, and the Scientific Revolution* (San Francisco: Harper & Row, 1980), 1.

4   Ibid., xvii.

5   Ibid., 27.

6   Sharon O'Dair points us in this direction in '"To Fright the Animals and To Kill Them Up": Shakespeare and Ecology'. *Shakespeare Studies* 39 (2011): 74–83.

7   Merchant, *The Death of Nature*, 5. See also Bruckner, 'N/nature and the Difference "She" Makes', 15–36.

8   Merchant, *The Death of Nature*, 42.

9   Ibid.

10 For an argument about such theoretical marginalization, see Natasha Korda, 'Shakespeare's Laundry', in *Rethinking Feminism: Gender, Race, and Sexuality in Early Modern*

    Studies, eds Ania Loomba and Melissa Sanchez (New York: Routledge, 2016).

11 Bruckner, 'N/nature and the Difference "She" Makes', 30.

12 Merchant, *The Death of Nature*, 67–8.

13 Rosi Braidotti, *Transpositions* (Maiden: Polity, 2006), 137; see also Alaimo, 'Sustainable This, Sustainable That', 558–64.

14 See Alaimo, *Bodily Natures*, 20.

15 See in particular ibid.; Barad, *Meeting the Universe Halfway*; Haraway, *When Species Meet;* and Plumwood, 'Nature in the Active Voice'.

16 See Jeremy Davies, 'Sustainable Nostalgia'. *Memory Studies* 3 (no. 3) (April 2010): 264.

17 Catchmay, 'A Booke of Medicens', fol. 28r.

18 See the following article about a 2008 exhibit at the Smithsonian. Janet Raloff, 'Dirt is Not Soil'. *Science News: Magazine of the Society for Science and the Public*, 17 July 2008. https://www.sciencenews.org/blog/science-public/dirt-not-soil (accessed 6 May 2016).

19 Catchmay, 'A Booke of Medicens', fol. 12r.

20 Ibid.

21 See Barad, *Meeting the Universe Halfway*, where she writes, 'intra-action' 'signifies the mutual constitution of entangled agencies' (33).

22 See Chapter 2 of Phyllis Rackin's *Shakespeare and Women* (Oxford: Oxford University Press, 2005), 26–47. See also Natasha Korda, *Shakespeare's Domestic Economies: Gender and Property in Early Modern England* (Philadelphia: University of Pennsylvania Press, 2002), Korda, *Labors Lost*; Wall, *Staging Domesticity*; and Wall, *Recipes For Thought*.

23 Mary O'Connor and Sara Mendelson, 'Foreword: Sylvia Bowerbank (1947–2005); in *Ecofeminist Approaches to Early Modernity*, eds Jennifer Munroe and Rebecca Laroche (New York: Palgrave Macmillan, 2011), xiii–xvii.

24 See especially Chapter 6, 'Preserving the Earth: Women and the Progressive Conservation Movement', in Carolyn Merchant,

Earthcare: Women and the Environment (Abingdon and New York: Routledge, 2013 [1996]), 109–38.
25 Sturgeon, *Ecofeminist Natures*, 1.
26 http://www.makingandknowing.org/ (accessed 5 May 2016).
27 http://rarecooking.com/ (accessed 5 May 2016).

Appendix

1 DiMeo and Laroche, 'On Elizabeth Isham's "Oil of Swallows"', 87–104.
2 Anonymous, 'Commonplace Book and Recipe Book', University of Pennsylvania MS Codex 823.
3 http://luna.folger.edu/luna/servlet/FOLGERCM1~6~6. To access all images, enter 'receipt books' into the search window (accessed 2 September 2016).
4 http://shakespeare.folger.edu (accessed 2 September 2016).
5 See https://www.shakespearesworld.org/#/ for the main website and https://blog.shakespearesworld.org/ for the ongoing blog series related to the project (accessed 2 September 2016).
6 See EMROC's website for its Mission Statement: emroc.hypotheses.org (accessed 7 September 2016).

BIBLIOGRAPHY

Adams, Rebecca. 'Body Shame May Actually Be Making Women Sick, Study Suggests'. *Huffington Post*, 4 August 2015. Available online: http://www.huffingtonpost.com/entry/body-shame-may-be-making-women-sick_us_55c0c54be4b06363d5a363db? (accessed 5 May 2016).

Alaimo, Stacy. *Bodily Natures: Science, Environment, and the Material Self*. Bloomington: Indiana University Press, 2010.

Alaimo, Stacy. 'Sustainable This, Sustainable That: The New Materialisms, Posthumanism, and Unknown Futures'. *PMLA* 127 (no. 3) (2012): 558–564.

Alaimo, Stacy. *Undomesticated Ground: Recasting Nature as Feminine Space*. Ithaca: Cornell University Press, 2000.

Andreou, Alex. 'Anti-Homeless Spikes: "Sleeping Rough Opened My Eyes to the City's Barbed Cruelty"'. *Guardian*, 18 February 2015. Available online: http://www.theguardian.com/society/2015/feb/18/defensive-architecture-keeps-poverty-unseen-and-makes-us-more-hostile (accessed 4 May 2016).

Anonymous. *A Closet for Ladies and Gentlewomen*. London: 1608.

Anonymous. 'Cookery books: 17th/18th century'. Wellcome MS 1795.

Anonymous. 'Commonplace Book and Recipe Book', University of Pennsylvania MS Codex 823.

Anonymous. 'Medical and Cooking Recipes'. Bryn Mawr MS 19.

Archer, Jayne et al. 'The Autumn King: Remembering the Land in *King Lear*'. *Shakespeare Quarterly* 63 (no. 4) (Winter 2012): 518–43.

Aubrey, Allison. 'From Ugly to Hip: Misfit Fruits and Veggies Coming to Whole Foods'. 7 March 2016. Available online: http://www.npr.org/sections/thesalt/2016/03/07/469530045/from-ugly-to-hip-misfit-fruits-and-veggies-coming-to-whole-foods (accessed 5 May 2016).

Bacon, Sir Francis. *The New Organon Or: True Directions Concerning the Interpretation of Nature*, Book 1, Aphorism 1. Available online: http://www.earlymoderntexts.com/assets/pdfs/bacon1620.pdf (accessed 2 May 2016).

Baker, Margaret. 'Receipt Book of Margaret Baker'. Folger MS 619.

Ballantyne, Coco. 'Strange But True: Antibacterial Products May Do More Harm Than Good'. *Scientific American*, 7 June 2007. Available online: http://www.scientificamerican.com/article/strange-but-true-antibacterial-products-may-do-more-harm-than-good/ (accessed 3 May 2016).

Barad, Karen. 'Posthumanist Performativity: Toward an Understanding of How Matter Comes to Matter'. *Signs: Journal of Women in Culture and Society* 28 (no. 3) (2003): 801–31.

Barad, Karen. *Meeting the Universe Halfway: Quantum Physics and the Entanglement of Matter and Meaning*. Durham: Duke University Press, 2007.

Barkan, Leonard. '"Living Sculptures": Ovid, Michelangelo, and *The Winter's Tale*'. *ELH* 48.4, 1981: 639–67.

Bennett, Jane. *Vibrant Matter: A Political Ecology of Things*. Durham and London: Duke University Press, 2010.

Bland, Archie. 'Should We Wipe Mosquitos Off the Face of the Earth'. *Guardian*, 10 February 2016. Available online: http://www.theguardian.com/global/2016/feb/10/should-we-wipe-mosquitoes-off-the-face-of-the-earth (accessed 2 May 2016).

Blum, Abbie. '"Strike All That Look Upon With Mar[b]le": Monumentalizing Women in Shakespeare's Plays'. In *The Englishwoman in Print: Counterbalancing the Canon*, edited by Anne M. Haselkorn and Betty S. Travitsky, 99–118 (Amherst: University of Massachusetts Press, 1990).

Boehrer, Bruce. 'The Privy and Its Double: Scatology and Satire in Shakespeare's Theater'. In *The Blackwell Companion to Shakespeare: The Poems, Problem Comedies, and Late Plays*, edited by Jean Howard and Richard Dutton, 69–88. Oxford: Blackwell Press, 2003.

Bogost, Ian. *Alien Phenomenology; or What It's Like to Be a Thing*. Minneapolis and London: University of Minnesota Press, 2012.

Borlik, Todd. *Ecocriticism and Early Modern Literature: Green Pastures*. New York: Routledge, 2011.

Borlik, Todd. 'Fairy-Lore as Folk Entomology in Shakespeare's

England'. In *Performing Animals*, edited by Karen Raber (Forthcoming: Penn State University Press).

Botelho, Keith. *Little Beasts: Cultures of the Hive in Renaissance England*. (Yet unpublished monograph).

Bowerbank, Sylvia. *Speaking for Nature: Women and Ecologies of Early Modern England*. Baltimore and London: Johns Hopkins University Press, 2004.

Boyle Family. 'Recipe Book'. Wellcome MS 1340.

Braidotti, Rosi. *Transpositions*. Maiden: Polity, 2006.

Brown, Sarah Annes. 'Queering Pygmalion: Ovid, Euripides and *The Winter's Tale*'. In *Shakespeare's Erotic Mythology and Ovidian Renaissance Culture*, edited by Agnès Lafont, 139–52. Farnham: Ashgate, 2013.

Bruckner, Lynne Dickson. 'N/nature and the Difference "She" Makes'. In *Ecofeminist Approaches to Early Modernity*, edited by Jennifer Munroe and Rebecca Laroche, 15–36. New York: Palgrave Macmillan, 2011.

Bruckner, Lynne Dickson and Dan Brayton, eds. *Ecocritical Shakespeare*. Farnham: Ashgate, 2011.

Brumwich, Anne et al. 'Her Book of Receipts or Medicines'. Wellcome MS 160.

Caldecott, Leonie and Stephanie Leland, eds. *Reclaim the Earth: Women Speak Out for Life on Earth*. London: The Women's Press, 1983.

Callaghan, Dympna. *Shakespeare Without Women: Representing Gender and Race on the Renaissance Stage*. New York: Routledge, 2000.

Callaghan, Dympna. 'Confounded by Winter: Speeding Time in Shakespeare's Sonnets'. In *A Companion to Shakespeare's Sonnets*, edited by Michael Schoenfeldt, 104–18. Chichester: Wiley-Blackwell, 2010.

Campana, Joseph. 'The Bee and the Sovereign: Political Entomology and the Problem of Scale'. *Shakespeare Studies*, 41, 2013: 94–113.

Carson, Rachel. *Silent Spring*. Boston: Houghton Mifflin, 2002 [1962].

Catchmay, Lady Frances. 'A Booke of Medicens'. Wellcome MS 184a.

Chen, Mel. *Animacies: Biopolitics, Racial Mattering, and Queer Affect*. Durham and London: Duke University Press, 2012.

Cohen, Jeffrey. *Stone: An Ecology of the Inhuman*. Minneapolis: University of Minneapolis Press, 2015.
Coorsh, Karolyn. 'Would You Buy Ugly Vegetables? That's How a Grocery Chain Fights Waste', 29 July 2014. Available online: http://www.ctvnews.ca/world/would-you-buy-ugly-vegetables-that-s-how-a-grocery-chain-fights-waste-1.1938024 (accessed 5 May 2016).
Corlyon, Mrs. 'A Booke of diuers Medecines, Broothes, Salues, Waters, Syroppes and Oyntementes of which many or the most part haue been experienced and tryed by the speciall practize of Mrs Corlyon. Anno Domini 1606.' Folger MS v.a.388, f.1.
Couch, Robbie. 'Artists Got Fed Up With These "Anti-Homeless Spikes." So They Made Them a Bit More ... Comfy'. *Upworthy*, 24 July 2015. Available online: http://www.upworthy.com/artists-got-fed-up-with-these-anti-homeless-spikes-so-they-made-them-a-bit-more-comfy?c=ufb1 (accessed 4 May 2016).
Daston, Loraine. 'The Nature of Nature in Early Modern Europe'. *Configurations* 6 (1998): [Abridged 1–11] 149–72. Available online: http://isites.harvard.edu/fs/docs/icb.topic1360696.files/Daston-Nature%20of%20Nature%20abr.pdf (accessed 5 June 2015).
Daston, Loraine and Katharine Park, eds. *Wonders and the Order of Nature*. New York: Zone, 1998.
Davies, Jeremy. 'Sustainable Nostalgia'. *Memory Studies* 3 (no. 3) (April 2010): 262–8.
Davion, Victoria. "Is Ecofeminism Ecofeminist?" In *Ecological Feminism*, edited by Karen Warren, 8–28. New York: Routledge, 1994.
DiMeo, Michelle and Rebecca Laroche. 'On Elizabeth Isham's "Oil of Swallows": Animal Slaughter and Early Modern Women's Medical Recipes'. In *Ecofeminist Approaches to Early Modernity*, edited by Jennifer Munroe and Rebecca Laroche, 87–104. New York: Palgrave Macmillan, 2011.
Duckert, Lowell. 'Exit, Pursued by a Polar Bear (More to Follow)'. *Upstart*, 4 June 2013. Available online: http://www.clemson.edu/upstart/Essays/exit-pursued-by-a-polar-bear/exit-pursued-by-a-polar-bear.xhtml (accessed 30 November 2015).
d'Eaubonne, Françoise. *La Feminisme ou la Mort*. Paris: Pierre Horay, 1974.

Egan, Gabriel. 'Animals in Shakespearean Ecocriticism'. In *Shakespeare and Ecocritical Theory*, 95–119 (London: Bloomsbury/Arden, 2015).

Ellerbeck, Erin. 'Adoption and the Language of Horticulture in *All's Well That Ends Well*'. *SEL* 51 (no. 2) (2011): 305–26.

Estok, Simon. *Ecocriticism and Shakespeare: Reading Ecophobia*. New York: Palgrave, 2011.

Evelyn, John. 'Journal entry, September 3, 1666'. Reproduced by D. S. Grey in *Samuel Pepys' Diary*. Available online: http://www.pepys.info/fire.html (accessed 12 May 2016).

Feerick, Jean and Vin Nardizzi, eds. *The Indistinct Human in Renaissance Literature*. New York: Palgrave Macmillan, 2012.

Ferdman, Roberto A. 'France is Making it Illegal for Supermarkets to Throw Away Edible Food'. *Washington Post*, 22 May 2015. Available online: https://www.washingtonpost.com/news/wonk/wp/2015/05/22/france-is-making-it-illegal-for-supermarkets-to-throw-away-edible-food/ (accessed 5 May 2016).

Field, Catherine. '"Sweet Practicer, Thy Physic I Will Try": Helena and Her "Good Receipt" in *All's Well That Ends Well*'. In *All's Well That Ends Well: Critical Essays*, edited by Gary Waller, 194–208. New York and London: Routledge, 2007.

Floyd-Wilson, Mary. *Occult Knowledge, Science, and Gender on the Shakespearean Stage*. Cambridge: Cambridge University Press, 2013.

Floyd-Wilson, Mary and Garrett Sullivan, eds. *Environment and Embodiment in Early Modern England*. Basingstoke, Hampshire and New York: Palgrave Macmillan, 2007.

Glotfelty, Cheryl and Harold Fromm, eds. *The Ecocriticism Reader: Landmarks in Literary Ecology*. Athens: University of Georgia Press, 1996.

Goldstein, David. 'Woolley's Mouse: Early Modern Recipe Books and the Uses of Nature'. In *Ecofeminist Approaches to Early Modernity*, edited by Jennifer Munroe and Rebecca Laroche, 105–28. New York: Palgrave Macmillan, 2011.

Gourlay, Patricia Southard. '"O My Most Sacred Lady": Female Metaphor in *The Winter's Tale*'. In *The Winter's Tale: Critical Essays*, edited by Maurice Hunt, 258–79. New York: Garland, 1995.

Gray, Elizabeth Dodson. *Green Paradise Lost*. Wellesley: Roundtable Press, 1979.

Grey, D. S., ed. *Samuel Pepys' Diary*. Available online: http://www.pepys.info/fire.html (accessed 20 November 2015).
Grey, Elizabeth (Countess of Kent). *A choice manual; or, Rare secrets in physic and chirurgery: collected, & practiced by the Right Honourable the Countess of Kent, late deceased*. London, 1653.
Griffin, Susan. *Woman and Nature: The Roaring Inside Her*. New York: Harper & Row, 1980.
Gross, Liz. 'Pollution, Poverty, and People of Color: Don't Drink the Water'. *Scientific American*, 12 June 2012. Available online: http://www.scientificamerican.com/article/pollution-poverty-people-color-dont-drink-water/ (accessed 5 May 2016).
Hackel, Heidi Brayman and Ian Frederick Moulton, eds. *Teaching Early Modern English Literature from the Archives*. New York: Modern Language Association of America, 2015.
Hamnet: Folger Library Catalog. Shakespeare.folger.edu.
Haraway, Donna. 'A Cyborg Manifesto' [1984]. Available online: http://faculty.georgetown.edu/irvinem/theory/Haraway-CyborgManifesto-1.pdf (accessed 21 September 2016).
Haraway, Donna. 'Situated Knowledges: The Science Question in Feminism and the Privilege of Partial Perspective'. *Feminist Studies* 14 (no. 3) (Autumn 1988): 575–99.
Haraway, Donna. *When Species Meet*. Minneapolis: University of Minnesota Press, 2008.
Haraway, Donna. 'Anthropocene, Capitalocene, Chthulucene: Staying with the Trouble', 9 May 2014. Available online: https://vimeo.com/97663518 (accessed 2 May 2016).
Heft, Harry. 'Affordances, Dynamic Experience, and the Challenge of Reification'. *Ecological Psychology* 15 (no. 2) (2003): 149–80. Available online: http://www.faculty.virginia.edu/perlab/misc/ReadingMeeting/Heft,2003.pdf (accessed 2 May 2016).
Höefele, Andreas. *Stage Stake, and Scaffold: Humans and Animals in Shakespeare's Theatre*. Oxford: Oxford University Press, 2011.
Hogan, Patrick G. Jr. 'Marvell's "Vegetable Love"'. *Studies in Philology* 60 (no. 1) (January 1963): 1–11.
Howard, Jean. 'Female Agency in *All's Well That Ends Well*'. *AUMLA: Journal of the Australasian Universities Modern Language and Literature Association* 106 (November 2006): 43–60.

Ingold, John. 'Decade After Hayman Fire, Questions Linger about Fire's Start'. *The Denver Post*, 3 June 2012. Available online: http://www.denverpost.com/ci_20769983/decade-after-hayman-fire-questions-linger-about-fires (accessed 3 May 2016).

Jacob, Elizabeth et al. 'Physicall and Chyrurgicall Receipts'. Wellcome MS 3009.

Johnson, Barbara. *Persons and Things*. Cambridge: Harvard University Press, 2008.

Johnson Family. 'Recipe Book'. Wellcome MS 3082.

Kellet, Katherine R. 'Petrarchan Desire, the Female Ghost, and *The Winter's Tale*'. In *Staging the Blazon in Early Modern English Theater*, edited by Deborah Uman and Sara Morrison, 25–36. Farnham: Ashgate, 2013.

Knight, Leah. *Reading Green in Early Modern England*. Farnham and Burlington: Ashgate, 2014.

Kolodny, Annette. *The Lay of the Land: Metaphor as Experience and History in American Life and Letters*. Chapel Hill: University of North Carolina Press, 1975.

Korda, Natasha. *Shakespeare's Domestic Economies: Gender and Property in Early Modern England*. Philadelphia: University of Pennsylvania Press, 2002.

Korda, Natasha. *Labors Lost: Women's Work in the Early Modern English Stage*. Philadelphia: University of Pennsylvania Press, 2011.

Korda, Natasha. 'Shakespeare's Laundry'. In *Rethinking Feminism: Gender, Race, and Sexuality in Early Modern Studies*, edited by Ania Loomba and Melissa Sanchez. New York: Routledge, 2016.

Lamont, J. 'Trait Body Shame Predicts Health Outcomes in College Women: A Longitudinal Investigation'. *Journal of Behavioral Medicine* 38 (no. 6) (December 2015): 998–1008.

Laroche, Rebecca. 'Ophelia's Plants and the Death of Violets' as well. In *Ecocritical Shakespeare*, edited by Lynne Bruckner and Dan Brayton, 211–22. Farnham: Ashgate, 2011.

Laroche, Rebecca. 'Roses in Winter: Recipe Ecologies and Shakespeare's Sonnets'. In *Ecological Approaches to Early Modern English Texts*, edited by Jennifer Munroe, Edward J. Geisweidt and Lynne Bruckner, 51–61. Farnham: Ashgate, 2015a.

Laroche, Rebecca. '"Cabbage and Roots" and the Difference of Merry Wives'. In *The Merry Wives of Windsor: New Critical*

Essays, edited by Evelyn Gajowski and Phyllis Rackin, 184–94. London and New York: Routledge, 2015b.

Laroche, Rebecca and Jennifer Munroe. 'On a Bank of Rue; Or Materialist Ecofeminist Inquiry and the Garden of *Richard II*'. *Shakespeare Studies* 42 (2014): 42–50.

Latour, Bruno. *We Have Never Been Modern*. Trans. Catherine Porter. Cambridge: Harvard University Press, 1993.

Layfielde, Anne. 'Recipe Book of Anne Layfielde'. College of Physicians of Philadelphia MS 10a214.

Leong, Elaine. 'Collecting Knowledge for the Family: Recipes, Gender and Practical Knowledge in the Early Modern English Household'. *Centaurus* 55 (no. 2) (1991): 81–103.

Leong, Elaine. 'Making Medicines in the Early Modern Household'. *Bulletin of the History of Medicine* 82 (no. 1) (2008): 145–68.

Leong, Elaine and Sara Pennell. 'Recipe Collections and the Currency of Medical Knowledge in the Early Modern "Medical Marketplace"'. In *Medicine and the Market in England and Its Colonies, c. 1450–c. 1850*, edited by M. S. Jenner, 133–52. Basingstoke: Palgrave Macmillan, 2007.

Leong, Elaine and Alicia Rankin, eds. *Secrets and Knowledge in Medicine and Science, 1500–1800*. Farnham: Ashgate, 2011.

Levine, Laura L. *Men in Women's Clothing: Anti-Theatricality and Effeminization, 1579–1642*. Cambridge: Cambridge University Press, 1994.

Longe, Sarah. 'A Booke of Receiptes', Folger MS v.a.425.

Lupton, Julia Reinhard. 'The Renaissance Res Publica of Furniture'. In *Animal, Vegetable, Mineral: Ethics and Objects*, edited by Jeffrey Jerome Cohen, 211–36. Washington: Oliphaunt, 2012.

Markham, Gervase. *The Second Booke of the English Husbandman*. London, 1614.

Markham, Gervase. *Country Contentments, or The English Huswife*. London, 1623. Available online: http://digital.library.lse.ac.uk/objects/lse:heh898zor (accessed 13 May 2016).

Martin, Randall. '"I Wish You the Joy Of the Worm": Evolutionary Ecology in *Hamlet* and *Antony and Cleopatra*.' In *Shakespeare and Ecology*, 134–65. Oxford: Oxford University Press, 2015.

McColley, Diane Kelsey. *Milton's Eve*. Urbana: University of Illinois Press, 1983.

Mentz, Steve. 'Strange Weather in King Lear'. *Shakespeare* 6, 2010: 139–52. Available online: http://stevementz.com/wp-content/uploads/2012/07/Strange-Weather-in-King-Lear.pdf (accessed 4 May 2016).

Mentz, Steve. 'After Sustainability'. *PMLA* 127 (no. 3) (May 2012): 586–92.

Merchant, Carolyn. *The Death of Nature: Women, Ecology, and the Scientific Revolution*. San Francisco: Harper & Row, 1980.

Merchant, Carolyn. *Earthcare: Women and the Environment*. Abingdon and New York: Routledge, 2013 [1996].

Millman, Oliver. 'Climate change may have helped spread Zika virus, according to WHO scientists'. *Guardian*, 11 February 2016. Available online: http://www.theguardian.com/world/2016/feb/11/climate-change-zika-virus-south-central-america-mosquitos (accessed 2 May 2016).

Moffat, Thomas. *Theatre of Insects, or the Lesser Living Creatures*, printed with Edward Topsel *The History of Four-Footed Beasts and Serpents*. London, 1658.

Moore, Jason. 'The Capitalocene, Part I: On the Nature and Origins of Our Ecological Crisis', 2014. Available online: http://www.jasonwmoore.com/uploads/The_Capitalocene__Part_I__June_2014.pdf (accessed 2 May 2016).

Moore, Jason. 'The Capitalocene, Part II: Abstract Social Nature and the Limits of Capital', 2014. Available online: http://www.jasonwmoore.com/uploads/The_Capitalocene___Part_II__June_2014.pdf (accessed 5 May 2016).

Morton, Timothy. 'Everything We Need: Scarcity, Scale, Hyper-Objects'. *Architectural Design* 82 (no. 4) (2012): 78–81.

Morton, Timothy. 'Treating Objects Like Women: Feminist Ontology and the Question of Essence'. In *International Perspectives in Feminist Ecocriticism*, edited by Greta Gaard, Serpil Opperman and Simon Estok, 56–69. New York and London: Routledge, 2013.

Munroe, Jennifer. *Gender and the Garden in Early Modern English Literature*. Burlington: Ashgate, 2008.

Munroe, Jennifer. 'First "Mother of Science": Milton's Eve, Knowledge, and Nature'. In *Ecofeminist Approaches to Early Modernity*, edited by Jennifer Munroe and Rebecca Laroche, 37–55. New York: Palgrave Macmillan, 2011a.

Munroe, Jennifer. '"It's all about the gillvors": Art and Nature in The Winter's Tale'. In *Ecocritical Shakespeare*, edited by Lynne Bruckner and Dan Brayton, 139–55. Farnham: Ashgate, 2011b.

Munroe, Jennifer. 'Is it Really Ecocritical If it Isn't Feminist?' In *Ecological Approaches to Early Modern Texts: A Field Guide to Reading and Teaching*, edited by Jennifer Munroe, Edward J. Geisweidt and Lynne Bruckner, 37–47. Aldershot and Burlington: Ashgate Press, 2015a.

Munroe, Jennifer. 'Shakespeare and Ecocriticism Reconsidered'. *Literature Compass* 12 (no. 9) (2015b): 37–50.

Munroe, Jennifer and Rebecca Laroche, eds. *Ecofeminist Approaches to Early Modernity*. New York: Palgrave, 2011.

Neely, Carol Thomas. *Distracted Subjects: Madness and Gender in Shakespeare and Early Modern Culture*. Ithaca: Cornell University Press, 2004.

Neimanis, Astrida, Cecilia Åsberg and Johan Hedrén. 'Four Problems, Four Directions for Environmental Humanities: Toward Critical Posthumanities for the Anthropocene'. *Ethics and the Environment* 20 (no. 1) (Spring 2015): 67–97.

Nikisch, Curt. 'Trader Joe's Ex-President Opens Store with Aging Food and Cheap Meals', 4 June 2015. Available online: http://www.npr.org/sections/thesalt/2015/06/04/411777947/trader-joes-ex-president-opens-store-with-aging-food-and-cheap-meals (accessed 5 May 2016).

Nixon, Rob. *Slow Violence and the Environmentalism of the Poor*. Cambridge, MA, and London: Harvard University Press, 2011.

Noble, Louise. '"Bare and Desolate Now": Cultural Ecology and "The Description of Cookham"'. In *Ecological Approaches to Early Modern Texts: A Field Guide to Reading and Teaching*, edited by Jennifer Munroe, Edward J. Geisweidt and Lynne Bruckner, 99–108. Aldershot and Burlington: Ashgate Press, 2015.

Nunn, Hillary. 'Elizabeth Downing's Busy Month of May'. *The Recipes Project*, 2014. Available online http://recipes.hypotheses.org/3776 (accessed 13 May 2016).

Nunn, Hillary. 'On Vegetating Virgins: Greensickness and the Plant Realm in Early Modern Literature'. In *The Indistinct Human in Renaissance Literature*, edited by Jean Feerick and Vin Nardizzi, 159–80. New York: Palgrave Macmillan, 2012.

Nuttall, A. D. '*The Winter's Tale*: Ovid Transformed'. In

Shakespeare's Ovid: The Metamorphoses in the Plays and Poems, edited by A. B. Taylor, 135–49. Cambridge: Cambridge University Press, 2000.

O'Connor, Mary and Sara Mendelson. 'Foreword: Sylvia Bowerbank (1947–2005)'. In *Ecofeminist Approaches to Early Modernity*, edited by Jennifer Munroe and Rebecca Laroche, xiii–xvii. New York: Palgrave Macmillan, 2011.

O'Dair, Sharon. '"To Fright the Animals and To Kill Them Up": Shakespeare and Ecology'. *Shakespeare Studies* 39 (2011): 74–83.

Oxford English Dictionary. Available online: http://www.oed.com/ (accessed 13 May 2016).

Pennell, Sara. 'Pots and Pans History: The Material Culture of the Kitchen in Early Modern England'. *Journal of Design History* 11 (no. 3) (1998): 201–16.

Phillips, Suzanne. *Hidden Killers of the Tudor Home*. London: BBC, 2015 (film).

Plat, Hugh. *Floraes Paradise*. London, 1608.

Plumwood, Val. *Feminism and the Mastery of Nature*. London: Routledge, 1993.

Plumwood, Val. *Environmental Culture: The Ecological Crisis of Reason*. Abingdon: Routledge, 2002.

Plumwood, Val. 'Nature in the Active Voice'. *Australian Humanities Review* 46 (May 2009). Available online: http://www.australianhumanitiesreview.org/archive/Issue-May-2009/plumwood.html (accessed 13 May 2016)

Pollan, Michael. *The Botany of Desire*. New York: Random House, 2001.

Pollan, Michael. 'Some of My Best Friends Are Germs'. *New York Times Magazine*, 15 May 2013. Available online: http://www.nytimes.com/2013/05/19/magazine/say-hello-to-the-100-trillion-bacteria-that-make-up-your-microbiome.html?pagewanted=all&_r=0 (accessed 3 May 2016).

Proudfoot, Richard, Ann Thompson and David Scott Kastan, eds. *The Arden Shakespeare Complete Works*. London and New York: Bloomsbury Arden, 2014 [1998].

Raber, Karen. *Animal Bodies, Renaissance Culture*. Philadelphia: University of Pennsylvania Press, 2013.

Rackin, Phyllis. *Shakespeare and Women*. Oxford: Oxford University Press, 2005.

Raloff, Janet. 'Dirt is Not Soil'. *Science News: Magazine of the Society for Science and the Public*, 17 July 2008. Available online: https://www.sciencenews.org/blog/science-public/dirt-not-soil (accessed 6 May 2016).

Rico, Barbara Roche. 'From "Speechless Dialect" to "Prosperous Art": Shakespeare's Recasting of the Pygmalion Image'. *Huntington Library Quarterly* 48 (no. 3) (1985): 285–95.

Roberts, Jeanne Addison. *The Shakespearean Wild: Geography, Genus, and Gender*. Lincoln and London: University of Nebraska Press, 1994.

Robertson, Kellie. 'Abusing Aristotle'. In *Speculative Medievalisms: Discography*, edited by Eileen A. Joy, Anna Klosowska, Nicola Masciandro and Michael O'Rourke, 159–72. New York: Punctum, 2013. Available online: https://www.academia.edu/10235881/Abusing_Aristotle (accessed 5 May 2016).

Rosenberg, Jessica. 'Poetic Language, Practical Handbooks, and the "Vertues" of Plants'. In *Ecological Approaches to Early Modern English Texts*, edited by Jennifer Munroe, Edward J. Geisweidt and Lynne Bruckner, 61–70. Farnham: Ashgate, 2015.

Rosenberg, Jessica. 'The Point of the Couplet: Shakespeare's Sonnets and Tusser's *A Hundreth Good Points of Husbandrie*'. *ELH* 83 (no. 1) (Spring 2016): 1–41.

Royal Shakespeare Company. *The Taming of the Shrew: Live from Shakespeare's Globe*. New York: Films Media Group, c. 2012 [2013].

Ruether, Rosemary Radford. *New Woman/New Earth: Sexist Ideologies and Human Liberation*. New York: Seabury Press, 1975.

Schalkwyk, David. *Speech and Performance in Shakespeare's Sonnets and Plays*. Cambridge: Cambridge University Press, 2002.

Shannon, Laurie. *The Accommodated Animal: Cosmopolity in Shakespearean Locales*. Chicago: University of Chicago Press, 2013.

Shiva, Vandana. *Staying Alive: Women, Ecology, and Development*. Brooklyn and Boston: South End Press, 2010 [1988].

Somerville, Madeleine. 'Inequality of Environmentalism: Is Green Movement Exclusionary By Nature?' *Guardian*, 26 April 2016. Available online: http://www.theguardian.com/lifeandstyle/2016/

apr/26/environmentalism-inequality-farmers-market-go-green (accessed 13 May 2016).
Spenser, Edmund. *Edmund Spenser's Poetry: A Norton Critical Edition*, 4th edn, edited by Anne Lake Prescott and Andrew D. Hadfield. New York: W. W. Norton & Co., 2014.
Sturgeon, Noël. *Ecofeminist Natures: Race, Gender, Feminist Theory, and Political Action*. New York and London: Routledge, 1997.
Talbot, Aletheia (Countess of Arundell). *Natura Exenterata: or, Nature unbowelled by the most exquisite anatomizers of her*. London, 1655.
Thynne, Maria. 'Letters'. In *Lay by your Needles Ladies, Take the Pen: Writing Women in England, 1500–1700*, edited by Suzanne Trill, Kate Chedgzoy and Melanie Osborne, 76–77. London: St. Martin's Press, 1997.
Tigner, Amy. 'Preserving Nature in Hannah Woolley's *The Queen-Like Closet; or Rich Cabinet*'. In *Ecofeminist Approaches to Early Modernity*, edited by Jennifer Munroe and Rebecca Laroche, 87–104. New York: Palgrave Macmillan, 2011.
Tigner, Amy. *Literature and the Renaissance Garden from Elizabeth I to Charles II*. Burlington: Ashgate, 2012.
Trapnel, Anna. *The Cry of a Stone* (London, 1654). Women Writers Online, http://www.wwp.northeastern.edu/wwo/ (accessed 15 August 2015).
Traub, Valerie, M., Lindsay Kaplan and Dympna Callaghan, eds. *Feminist Readings of Early Modern Culture: Emerging Subjects*. Cambridge: Cambridge University Press, 1996.
Vickers, Nancy. 'Diana Described: Scattered Women, Scattered Rhymes'. In *Writing and Sexual Difference*, edited by Elizabeth Abel, 95–109. Chicago: University of Chicago Press, 1982.
Waldron, Jennifer. 'Of Stones and Stony Hearts: Desdemona, Hermione, and Post-Reformation Theater'. In *The Indistinct Human in Renaissance Literature*, edited by Jean E. Feerick and Vin Nardizzi, 205–27. New York: Palgrave Macmillan, 2012.
Wall, Wendy. *Staging Domesticity: Household Work and English Identity in Early Modern Drama*. Cambridge: Cambridge University Press, 2002.
Wall, Wendy. *Recipes for Thought: Knowledge and Taste in the*

Early Modern English Kitchen. Philadelphia: University of Pennsylvania Press, 2015.

Warren, Karen J., ed. 'Feminism and Ecology: Making Connections.' *Environmental Ethics* 9 (no. 1) (1987): 3–20.

Warren, Karen J., ed. *Ecological Feminism*. New York: Routledge, 1994.

Wescott, David. 'Survival of the Fittest in the English Department'. *The Chronicle of Higher Education*, 1 May 2015. Available online: http://chronicle.com/article/Jonathan-Gottschalls-Fighting/229763/ (accessed 4 May 2016).

Woolley, Hannah. *The Accomplisht Ladys Delight*. London, 1686.

Woolley, Hannah. *The Queen-Like Closet*. London, 1670.

Woolley, Hannah. *Supplement to the Queen-Like Closet*. London, 1674. Online at http://www.wwp.northeastern.edu/wwo/ (accessed 7 September 2016).

Yates, Julian. 'Macbeth's Bubbles'. Shakespeare Association of America. New Orleans, 26 March 2016.

INDEX

actors 120, 122
adoption 119–20
affordances 29–30, 107–8
agribusiness 61
Alaimo, Stacy 7, 10, 28, 42, 57, 58–9, 136
   Bodily Natures 19, 28, 42
   Multiple Chemical Sensitivity and 59
   'Sustainable This, Sustainable That' 149 n.16
   transcorporeality and 28, 42, 57, 58–9, 78, 82
   Undomesticated Ground: Recasting Nature as Feminine Space 4–5, 10
animal studies 43–4
animals 43–5 *see also* insects; pests
   ape 125
   Barbary cock-pigeon 124
   bear 43
   cats 44, 52, 53–8, 98
   cows/calves 49
   deer 43 *see also* hart under animals
   dog 69
   falcons 46
   hart 44 *see also* deer under animals
   horses 43
   lions 43, 51
   mice 20, 51–3, 57, 62
   monkey 125
   panther 44
   parrot 125
   rats 44, 45
   swallows 126
   toad 98
Anthropocene 8, 25
archives 139–40, 142, 143–6
Aristotle 117

Bacon, Francis 23, 131, 133
bacteria 61–2
ballads 55–6
Ballantyne, Coco 157 n.40
Barad, Karen 7–8, 136
Barkan, Leonard 107
Barton, Terry Lynn 74
beauty 121, 128–30 *see also* Petrarchism
Bennett, Jane 22, 23, 28, 106, 159 n.10
   Vibrant Matter 28
Bland, Archie 36
   'Should we wipe mosquitoes off the face of the Earth?' 35–6
Boehrer, Bruce 161 n.28
Bogost, Ian: *Alien Phenomenology* 29, 106
Borlik, Todd 44, 79

Botelho, Keith 44
boundaries 18–20, 30, 31, 40, 139 *see also* thresholds
    holes 45
    penetration and 41–2, 44, 45–51, 57, 139 *see also* pest control
    walls 41–2, 45–6
Bowerbank, Sylvia 52, 141
    Speaking for Nature: Women and Ecologies of Early Modern England 11–12, 132
Boyle, Robert 52
Braidotti, Rosi 134
Brooks, Daniel 35
Bruckner, Lynne: 'N/nature and the Difference "She" Makes' 12
Brumwich, Anne: 'Medicine to kill any Quick thinge as flye or flea that is crept into *the* eare, A' (recipe) 58

Caldecott, Leonie: *Reclaim the Earth* 3
Callaghan, Dympna 165 n.25
Campana, Joseph 44
Capitalocene 8–9, 159 n.10
Carson, Rachel: *Silent Spring* 3
Catchmay, Lady Francis 32, 33, 93–5, 96, 97, 135, 136–9
chaos xv
Chthulucene 25
climate change 34–5, 39–40, 74, 132
Closet for Ladies and Gentlewomen, A 64

Cohen, Jeffrey Jerome 110
colonial expansion 132, 133
Connell, Alyssa and Marissa Nicosia: 'Cooking the Archive' series 142
consumerism 32, 141
containment 19–22
cooking and ingredients 13–15, 21, 63–5 *see also* recipe books
    Macbeth and 101–2
    'To Candy all sorts of flowers, fruits, and spices, the cleare rocke Candy' (recipe) 64
Corlyon, Mrs 84–5, 94, 162 n.33
cosmetic industry 128
'Coy Damousel Conquered; or, the Couragious Gallants Uictory, The' (ballad) 56
cross-dressing 122
cultural materialism 116–17

Daston, Lorraine 25, 102
databases *see* archives
Davies, Jeremy 136
Davion, Victoria 3
Day, Simon Paisley 54
Descartes, René 131
DiMeo, Michelle 12
dirt 126–7
domestic sphere, the 18–22, 57–8, 62–3 *see also* gardens; households
    penetration and 41–2, 44, 45–51, 57 *see also* pest control
    walls 41–2, 45–6

INDEX

wild, and the 40–1, 42–3
domination, forms of 3–4

Early English Books Online
  (EEBO) 144–5
Early Modern Animal Studies
  43–4
Early Modern Letters Online
  (EMLO) 144
Early Modern Manuscripts
  Online (EMMO) project
  144
Early Modern Recipes Online
  Collection (EMROC)
  145–6
earth 136–7
earth goddess 9
d'Eaubonne, Françoise:
  *Feminism ou la Mort,
  La* 2
EBBA (English Broadside
  Ballad Archive) 144
ecocriticism 1
ecofeminism v–xvi, 2–3
  early modern studies 11–14
  as lived practice 140–2
'Ecofeminist Perspectives:
  Culture, Nature, Theory'
  conference 2
ecophobia 43
EEBO (Early English Books
  Online) 144–5
eggs 138–9
Ellerbeck, Erin 119
embeddedness 20, 23–6, 78,
  79, 83, 88, 97–9, 102,
  103, 136
EMLO (Early Modern Letters
  Online) 144
EMMO (Early Modern
  Manuscripts Online)
  project 144
EMROC (Early Modern
  Recipes Online
  Collection) 145–6
enclosure 20–1
endosymbiotic relationships
  25–6
English Broadside Ballad
  Archive (EBBA) 144
environmental justice 88
environmentalism 2–3, 128–9
  see also climate change;
  sustainability
  feminism and 2–3, 5, 9
erotica 57
essentialism 9–10
Estok, Simon 12, 43, 160 n.20
  see also ecophobia
Evelyn, John 66
'Excellent good and approued
  Oyntement, for all
  maner of Aches, Agues,
  Bruses, Goutes, Cankers,
  Lamenes, Stitches, or
  hardenes of the Spleene,
  and for all maner of
  paine in the Heade
  and Eares, An' (recipe)
  64–5

fear 43–4, 51–2
  fire and 63, 70–4
feminism 2–3, 109
  environmentalism and 2–3,
    5, 9
  materialist feminism 6–7
  Winter's Tale, The and 107
Field, Catherine 93, 161 n.25
fire 19, 21, 40–1, 53, 63–73

Great Fire of London 65, 66, 72
Hayman fire, Colorado 73–5
war and 71–2
fistulas 92–4, 161 n.25
Floyd-Wilson, Mary 25, 27, 90–1
Folger Shakespeare Library 144
food 128–9
France 129
Freccero, John 164 n.14

gardens 45–9, 60–1, 111–12, 116, *see also* plants
maintenance of 115
Plat, Hugh and 114, 115
gender 46–50
All's Well That Ends Well 119
cats and 54–5, 58
knowledge and 85–6, 103–4
Macbeth and 99, 100
performance and 122
recipes and 86
subjectivity and 26–8, 30–1
Winter's Tale, The 70, 106–7
Gerard, John 161 n.24
'Golden Oyle, The' (recipe) 112
Goldstein, David 12–13, 52–3
Gottschall, Jonathan 103–4
grace 113
Gray, Elizabeth Dodson: *Green Paradise Lost* 3
Great Fire of London, the 65–7

Haraway, Donna 25, 77, 85–6, 90, 136, 159 n.9
'Anthropocene, Capitalocene, Cthulucene' 152 n.18
'Cyborg Manifesto, A' 4
'Situated Knowledges' 86
harmony xvii–xviii
Harvey, William 131
'Have Among You Good Women' (ballad) 56
Hayman fire, Colorado 73–5
Heft, Harry 29–30, 31, 107–8, 111
Henry V (king of England) 72
Hobbes, Thomas 131
holes 45
homelessness 159 n.11
honey 84, 139
household work 13–15, 34
see also cooking and ingredients; domestic sphere, the
households 20–1, 33, 47–8 *see also* domestic sphere, the; pests
fire and 63–73
thresholds and 33
housewives 21, 48–9, 50 *see also* women
Howard, Jean 119
human–nonhuman relationships xiv, 104, 108, 130, 134–40
All's Well That Ends Well 89–93, 95–8, 119–20
King Lear 78–84, 86–9
language and 113–14
Macbeth 98–103
medicine and 84–5, 94–5
performance and 122
Twelfth Night 124

INDEX

Humanities, the 103–4, 144
humans 8 *see also*
   transcorporeality
   knowledge and 23–4
   plants and 21
husbands 48–9

identity 26 *see also*
   self-fashioning
indigenous knowledge practice 132, 133
industrialization 8, 132
inequalities xvii, 8–9
insects *see also* pests
   ants 60–1
   bees 62, 139
   butterflies 62
   crickets 44
   fly 34, 45, 58, 62, 127
   fleas, flies and creeping creatures 58–63
   mosquitoes 35–6
   moths 44, 45, 48, 49–50
   spiders 33, 44
   wasps 44
   worms 50, 61
intimacy 133–4

Johnson, Barbara 106

Kent, Countess of: *Choice Manual, A* 145
Knight, Leah 110, 164 n.17
knowledge 22–6, 77–8
   All's Well That Ends Well 89–93, 95–8
   gender and 85–6, 103–4
   Humanities, and the 103
   King Lear 78–84, 86–9
   Macbeth 98–103

   making and knowing project 142
   plants and 113
   recipes and 86
   situated knowledge 86
   unknowability 89–98
Kolodny, Annette: *Lay of the Land: Metaphor as Experience and History in American Life and Letters, The* 1
Korda, Natasha 20, 33, 116, 140

land 4–5
   King Lear and 81–2, 88–9
Lanyer, Aemilia 13–14
Laroche, Rebecca 12, 13
Laroche, Rebecca and Jennifer Munroe
   Ecofeminist Approaches to Early Modernity 12–13
   'On a Bank of Rue' 13
Latour, Bruno 7, 159 n.10
Leland, Stephanie: *Reclaim the Earth* 3
linguistics 113–14
Linnaeus, Carl 113
literary Darwinism 103
love 125–6
LUNA digital image collection 14

McColley, Diane
   Milton's Eve 12
madness, *King Lear* and 86–7
making and knowing project 142
Markham, Gervase 133
   English Huswife, The 48–9, 50, 145

Second Book of The English Husbandman, The 45–9, 60
marriage 125
materialism 116–17
materialist feminism 6–7, 20
medicine 14–15, 21, 58–9 *see also* pest control
   All's Well That Ends Well and 89–93, 95–8, 161 n.25
   Catchmay, Lady Francis and 93–5, 138–9
   Corlyon, Mrs and 84–5
   human/nonhuman relationships and 84–5
   King Lear and 83–4
   plants and 31–2, 83–4, 113, 127
   rue and 116
   salves 57, 64–5
   spiders and 33
Mendelson, Sara 141
Mentz, Steve xvii, 82, 158 n.6
Merchant, Carolyn 131–4
   Death of Nature, The 3, 4
   Earthcare 141
micro-practices 134–5, 139
Millman, Oliver: 'Climate Change may have helped spread Zika virus according to WHO scientists' 34–5
Milton, John: *Paradise Lost* 13
miracles 96–7
Moffat, Thomas 44
monologic systems 4
Moore, Jason 5, 8–9, 159 n.10
Morton, Timothy 108
Munroe, Jennifer 13
   'First "Mother of Science": Milton's Eve' 13
   'Is it Really Ecocritical If it isn't Feminist?' 13
Munroe, Jennifer and Rebecca Laroche
   Ecofeminist Approaches to Early Modernity 12–13
   'On a Bank of Rue' 13

natural 23, 25, 160 n.19
natural resources 104
   exploitation of 128–9
nature 7, 92, 133, 134, 140–2
Neely, Carol 160 n.19
new materialism 27–8
Newton, Isaac 131
Nicosia, Marissa and Alyssa Connell: 'Cooking the Archive' series 142
nip 113–14
Noble, Louise 13–14
nosebleeds 33
Nunn, Hillary: 'Elizabeth Downing's Busy Month of May' 112
   'On Vegetating Virgins' 14

Object Oriented Ontology (OOO) 46, 106, 124
objectification 109, 124, 127
objectivity 4, 6, 24, 85–6
   see also subject-object relations
objects 105–8
O'Connor, Mary 141
oikos 151 n.6
'Oil of Swallows' (recipe) 143
OOO (Object Oriented Ontology) 46, 106, 124

INDEX

Penn in Hand digitization project 144
Pepys, Samuel 65, 66, 72
perception 28–30
pest control
  cats and mice 51–8
  fleas, flies and creeping creatures 58–63
  'To destroy Moths, or drive them from the Cloth' (recipe) 50
  'To Kill Worms' (recipe) 61
pests 18–19, 45–9 *see also* pest control
  mice 51–3, 57, 62
  mosquitoes 35–6
  moths 44, 48, 49–50
  rats 50, 53
  spiders 33
  worms 59–61
Petrarchism 107–11, 113–15, 127, 128
Pine Tree Foundation 144
plants 108, 110–30, 136–7 *see also* gardens
  As You Like It and 121–2
  avens 94
  bay leaves 64
  bellamours, fictitious nature of 111, 116
  bramble 94
  bugle 94
  chamomile 136
  columbine 111
  comfrey 95
  cowslip 112
  cross-species impersonation of 122
  cuckoo-flowers 84
  cultivation 32
  daffodil 126–8
  daisies, including wild 84, 94
  darnel 84
  egremony 94
  embodiment and 117–28
  fennel 136
  fig 116
  fumitory 83, 136
  furrow-weeds 84
  garlic 47, 75
  gillyflowers 110
  grace and 113
  grass (three-leaved/white-spotted) 84, 85
  hemlock 84
  henbane 47
  herbs 47, 64
  human body and 21
  hyssop 136
  jasmine 111
  lily 111, 115, 116
  marigold 112, 136
  marjoram 116
  medicine and 31–2, 83–4, 127
  musk seed 50, 75
  nettles 84
  onion 47
  parsley 136
  personification of 118–28
  pinks 111
  pippin 60
  poetry and 110–13, 114–16
  primrose 112
  ribwort 94, 136
  rose 111, 114, 115, 118–19, 121–24
  rosemary 112, 136
  rue 64, 75, 116

sage 64
sanicle 94
scabies 94
seasonality and 112–13, 125, 126–7
seeds 45–7, 60
selfheal 136
speedwell 94
strawberry 111, 128
thyme 136
Titus Andronicus and 113–14
Twelfth Night and 121–2
violet (also viola) 112, 115, 116, 121–23, 127
walnut 116
Winter's Tale, The and 126–8
women and 117–27
wood betony 94
wormwood 64
Plat, Hugh 112
Floraes Paradise 114, 115
Plumwood, Val 23–4, 41, 57, 99–100, 124, 136
Environmental Culture 3, 4
Feminism and the Mastery of Nature 3
'Nature in the Active Voice' 3, 124, 149 n.17
poetry
blazon tradition 109, 110, 111, 116, 121
Petrarchism 107–11, 113–15, 127, 128
plants and 110–13, 114–16, 121
sonnets 27, 107, 110–13, 115, 116, 121, 126
Pollan, Michael 153 n.31
postcolonialism 133

posthumanism 6–9, 28, 106, 124
power relations 5–8, 10 *see also* status
All's Well That Ends Well and 90–3
As You Like It and 124–5
housewives and 21*King Lear* and 81–2
Winter's Tale, The and 126
preternatural 25, 102

Raber, Karen 44
Rackin, Phyllis 122, 140
rebellion 71–2
recipe books and recipes (receipts) 44, 50, 70, 97, 132, 134–40, 141
All's Well That Ends Well and 89–93, 95–8, 161 n.25
archives and 143–6
Brumwich, Anne and 58
Catchmay, Lady Francis and 33, 93–5, 135, 136–9
Corlyon, Mrs and 84–5, 162 n.33
'Excelent healinge drinke to cure, all mannor of wowndes, fistulaes, vlcers, in the bodye or owld soores, An' (recipe) 94
'Excellent good and approued Oyntement, for all maner of Aches, Agues, Bruses, Goutes, Cankers, Lamenes, Stitches, or hardenes of the Spleene, and for all maner of paine in the

Heade and Eares, An'
(recipe) 64–5
'For Kibed Heels' (recipe)
52–3
for stopping a nosebleed 33
gardens and 116
'Golden Oyle, The' (recipe)
112
Markham, Gervase and
45–6
'Medecine for a Pinn and a
Webb or any other soore
Eye, A' (recipe) 84
'Medicine to kill any Quick
thinge as flye or flea that
is crept into *th*e eare, A'
(recipe) 58
'Oil of Swallows' (recipe)
143
*Rich Storehouse, or
Treasury for the Disease,
A* 64–5
rue and 116
syrup of violets 127
Thynne, Maria and 116
'To Candy all sorts of
flowers, fruits, and
spices, the cleare rocke
Candy' (recipe) 64
'To destroy Moths, or drive
them from the Cloth'
(recipe) 50
'To Keep Away
moths Madam
Tyrwhitt's'(recipe) 49
'To Kill Rats' (recipe) 53
'To Kill Worms' (recipe) 61
Woolley, Hannah and 52–3
reproduction 119–20
Reuckert, William 1

Rich, Mary 52
*Rich Storehouse, or Treasury
for the Diseased, A* 64
Rico, Barbara Roche 107
Roberts, Jeanne Addison 42–3
*Shakespearean Wild:
Geography, Genius, and
Gender, The* 11
Rosenberg, Jessica 160 n.15,
165 n.25
Royal Shakespeare Company
54, 55, 56
Ruether, Rosemary Radford:
New Woman/New Earth
3

science 24, 85, 131–3
scientific discourse, early
modern 4, 85, 93, 113,
132
scientific methodology
103–4
scratching 53–7
'Scoulding Wife, The' 56
seasonality 112–13, 116, 125,
126–7
self-fashioning 26–7
Shakespeare, William
*All's Well That Ends
Well* 54–5, 67,
89–98, 118–20, 132,
161 n.25
As You Like It 74, 121–2,
124–5, 144
Coriolanus 54–5, 58–9, 69,
72
female characters 117–27,
130
gendered subjectivity
and 31

INDEX

Hamlet 44, 59–60, 61, 116, 117
Julius Caesar 71
King Henry IV, Part One 54
King Henry IV, Part Two 67–8, 71
King Henry V 68, 69, 72
King Henry VI, Part Two 71, 72
King Lear 34, 44, 51, 53, 59, 68, 69, 78–84, 86–8
King Richard II 13, 68, 71, 72
Love's Labour's Lost 44, 65
Macbeth 53, 71, 98–103, 110
Merchant of Venice, The 44
Merry Wives of Windsor, The 13, 68, 70
Midsummer Night's Dream, A 40, 43, 44, 51–2, 54, 59, 62, 63
Othello 27, 72–3
Pericles 41, 53
Richard II 71, 72
Romeo and Juliet 41, 53, 57, 121, 125, 132
sonnets 27, 107, 115, 116, 121
Taming of the Shrew, The 19, 54, 55–7, 67
Tempest, The 133
Titus Andronicus 13, 34, 43, 44, 62, 71, 113–14
Troilus and Cressida 70
Twelfth Night 109, 121–4, 132
Two Gentleman of Verona, The 69–70
Winter's Tale, The 70, 105–7, 109, 117, 122, 126–8
'Shakespeare's World' project 144
Shannon, Laurie 79
Shapiro, Samantha 54
Shiva, Vandana 4
  Staying Alive 133
situated knowledge 86, 102
skin 57
Smith, Pamela 142
sonnets 27, 107, 115, 116, 121
  see also Petrarchism
Spenser, Edmund 114, 116
  Amoretti 110–13, 115, 116
  Shepheardes Calender 114, 121
status 99–100
stone 105–7, 109–10, 122
storms 79, 80–3, 87
Sturgeon, Nöel 2, 141
subject-object relations 24–32, 100, 102, 105–8, 118–19 *see also* human-nonhuman relationship
subjectivity 6, 7 *see also* subject-object relations
  gendered 26–8, 30–1, 85
sugar 63–4
Sullivan, Garrett 27
supernatural 24, 25, 101, 160 n.19
sustainability xvii, 104, 135, 137

TCP-EEBO (Text Creation Partnership) 144–5
technology 104
Text Creation Partnership (TCP-EEBO) 144–5
thinking differently 124

thresholds 33–4, 139 *see also* boundaries
Thynne, Maria 116
Tigner, Amy 12
time 137 *see also* seasonality
'To Candy all sorts of flowers, fruits, and spices, the cleare rocke Candy' (recipe) 64
'To destroy Moths, or drive them from the Cloth' (recipe) 50
'To Keep Away moths Madam Tyrwhitt's'(recipe) 49
'To Kill Worms' (recipe) 61
transcorporeality 19, 28, 42, 57, 58–9, 78, 82, 83, 90
  King Lear and 78, 82, 86–7
Trapnel, Anna: *Cry of a Stone, The* 66

ugliness 129–30
University of Pennsylvania Rare Book and Manuscript Library 143–4
US 128–9

Vickers, Nancy J.: 'Diana Described' 109

Wall, Wendy 49, 71, 72, 101, 112, 140
  Recipes For Thought 158 n.52, 167 n.41
  Staging Domesticity 18, 20, 162 n.32
walls 41–2, 45–6 *see also* boundaries
war 71–2
Warren, Karen 5
  Ecological Feminism 3

waste 129–30
weather 79, 80–3, 87, 125, 126–7
Wellcome Library 143
WEMLO (Women's Early Modern Letters Online) 145
Whole Foods 129
wild, the 40–1, 42–5 *see also* cats
wildfires 65–7, 69–74
women 24 *see also* gender
  cats and 54–6
  desire and 120
  fire and 73–4
  housewives 21, 48–9, 50
  land and 4–5
  nature and 9–13
  nature metaphor and 118–20
  plants and 117–27
  scratching and 53–7
  virginity and 42, 45, 117
'Women and Life on Earth: Ecofeminism in the 1980s' conference 2
Women Writers Online (WWO) 144–5
Women's Early Modern Letters Online (WEMLO) 145
Woolley, Hannah 145
  'For Kibed Heels' (recipe) 52–3
  'To Kill Rats' (recipe) 53
Wroth, Lady Mary: *Pamphilia to Amphilanthus* 109
WWO (Women Writers Online) 144–5

Yates, Julian 161 n.29

Zika virus 33–6

www.ingramcontent.com/pod-product-compliance
Lightning Source LLC
Chambersburg PA
CBHW050139240426
43673CB00043B/1725